ENDORSEMENTS

"The *Family Philanthropy Navigator* is the breakthrough book of its domain. It's a must-read practical guide for families on their giving journey and an indispensable reference book for professionals in the domain."

Alexander Osterwalder, Co-Founder of Strategyzer and award-winning author of *Business Model Generation*.

"This is much more than a book: it is a practical and user-friendly tool – a must for all family philanthropists! The navigator will guide you step-by-step in your philanthropic journey, helping you to be more strategic, more impactful and to bring along other family members in a playful way, for the love of humanity."

Alexis du Roy de Blicquy, CEO of the Family Business Network (FBN).

"Business family owners have engaged in philanthropy with great enthusiasm and commitment over the years. Now, thanks to this timely book, they can count on a great tool to systematically and effectively respond to a growing need for non-profit support in society. This book is a practical and easy-to-use guide based on robust research, which will allow you to gain the confidence you need to thoughtfully contribute to making the world a better place."

André Hoffmann, Vice-Chairman, Roche Holding and President, MAVA Foundation.

"Good philanthropy is not as easy as it may seem. In my own experience meaningful philanthropy is a craft to be learnt. Education, curiosity, humility and passion is a must. The *Family Philanthropy Navigator* is a great place to start."

Astrid Kann-Rasmussen, Vice-Chair and Co-Founder of the KR Foundation and Chair of the V. Kann Rasmussen Foundation in the US.

"Family philanthropy has never looked so fun! Great ideas for the whole family to spend time on motives and values. A refreshing approach to the serious topic of giving."

Barbara Hauser, Editor-in-Chief, *The International Family Offices Journal*, Consulting Editor of Advising the Wealthy Client.

"At this very difficult time, the world needs more philanthropists that are committed to achieve positive change and long-lasting impact. The *Family Philanthropy Navigator* is a great tool for anyone who wants to ensure effective, impactful and meaningful giving."

Beatrice Fihn, Executive Director of ICAN, winner of the 2017 Nobel Peace Prize.

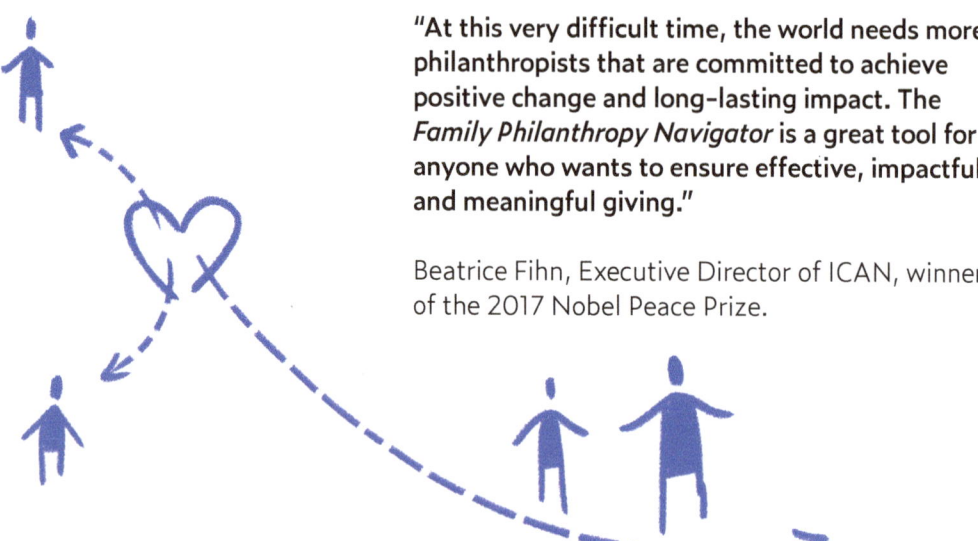

"Family philanthropy can be a key driving force for a more purpose-driven, sustainable and equitable world. This book is an excellent, to-the-point guide to navigate this important area. Highly recommended!"

Christian Busch, Director of the Global Economy program at New York University's Center for Global Affairs and author of *The Serendipity Mindset*.

"The Family Philanthropy Navigator is more than an inspiring and practical guidebook – although it is that for sure. This innovative book cleverly instigates a transformative process for families, a process that will clarify your philanthropic purpose as a family and help you build consensus around your goals and plans. This book is a gift."

John A. Davis, Faculty Leader of the MIT Family Enterprise Programs and Chairman of the Cambridge Family Enterprise Group.

"The family philanthropy journey can be daunting, but it doesn't have to be. The *Family Philanthropy Navigator* and its fun, hands-on activities provide practical tools any family can apply to their philanthropy effort."

Nick Tedesco, President and CEO at the National Center for Family Philanthropy.

"New realities bring new complexities that require new solutions. This book is a wonderful tool that helps families find a way to use their traditions and values to address today's global challenges through impactful philanthropy."

Ramia El Agamy, Editor-in-Chief, *Tharawat Magazine*.

"An illuminating take on how enterprising families can approach philanthropy to build impactful initiatives, along with business effectiveness and family cohesion. Activities and case studies provide a practical and fresh blueprint for any family thinking through their philanthropic strategy."

Rati Forbes, Director at Forbes Marshall and Forbes Marshall Foundation.

"The *Family Philanthropy Navigator* is a truly unique and engaging book. It is a definite must read for all family members of aspiring or established philanthropic families. It provides practical, easy-to-use and insightful tools that can be immediately implemented in your family's philanthropic activities."

Risto Väyrynen, Head of Family Business Community at the World Economic Forum.

Peter Vogel
Etienne Eichenberger
Małgorzata Kurak

FAMILY PHILANTHROPY NAVIGATOR

The Inspirational Guide
for Philanthropic Families
on Their Giving Journey

Chemin de Bellerive 23
P.O. Box 915
CH – 1001 Lausanne
Switzerland
Tel: +41 21 618 01 11 – Fax: +41 21 618 07 07
www.imd.org

All rights reserved. No part of this publication
may be reproduced, stored in a retrieval system,
or transmitted, in any form or by any means, electronic,
mechanical, photocopying, recording or otherwise,
without the prior written permission of IMD.

The right of Peter Vogel, Etienne Eichenberger
and Małgorzata Kurak to be identified as authors
of this work has been asserted by them in accordance
with the Copyright, Designs and Patents Act 1988.

Typeset in Zeitung Pro and Merriweather.
Zeitung Pro is a trademark of Underware; Merriweather
is licensed under SIL Open Font License, 1.1, Copyright
2016 The Merriweather Project Authors (https://github.
com/EbenSorkin/Merriweather), with Reserved Font
Name "Merriweather".

ISBN 978-2-940485-31-4
eISBN 978-2-940485-32-1

Designed by Housatonic.eu

x	**Acknowledgements**
xii	**Meet the Crew**
xiv	**Foreword**

1	**Get Ready for Your Philanthropic Journey**
2	The Need for a Family Philanthropy Navigator
12	Introducing the Navigator

23	**Purpose**
30	Motivation
42	Focus
56	Ambition
68	Case Studies

81	**Relationships**
88	Family Involvement
102	Partners
120	Case Studies

133	**Organization**
138	Resources
148	Governance
170	Impact
186	Case Studies

199	**Learning**

211	**Beyond the Navigator**
212	Beyond the Navigator
216	The Making of the Book

AKNOWLEDGEMENTS → thank you!

The creation of the *Family Philanthropy Navigator* has been a journey – during which we had the pleasure and opportunity to collaborate with, and get support from, a large number of individuals and organizations, who we would like to thank here.

Our sincere thanks go to the Mauvernay family and the Debiopharm Group, who made our dream of contributing to the field of family philanthropy possible by endowing the Debiopharm Chair for Family Philanthropy at IMD. Since the creation of the Chair back in September 2017, they have been tremendously supportive of our work and in particular the development of the *Family Philanthropy Navigator* toolkit and book.

We would also like to thank the other members of the crew who joined us in the journey of creating the *Family Philanthropy Navigator*. Matt Falloon, who with his enthusiasm, patience and editorial skills, has helped us successfully navigate the journey of writing this book. We would also like to thank the designers and illustrators Alfredo Carlo, Marcello Petruzzi and Beatrice Schena from the design agency Housatonic, who have not only helped us with the production of this book but have actually accompanied us throughout the entire process, and the many different workshops we conducted during the validation phase of the toolkit.

We would not have managed to arrive at this final product without the support of a number of amazing individuals who dedicated their time and effort supporting us in our various workshops, webinars or informal gatherings in order to provide us with their invaluable feedback and encourage us to deliver on the promise that we made: Allen Adler, Dr Dora Borenstein-Cognié, Régis Burrus, Matthew Crudgington, Ariane Duccor, Rati Forbes, Sabrina Grassi, Lynda Mansson, Loïc Pfister, Dr Patrick Reichert and Bernard Vischer. A special thanks goes to Alexander Osterwalder, who skillfully guided us at the beginning of our journey and helped us structure our process of writing and designing an insightful, visually appealing and user-friendly book.

We are immensely grateful to all the enterprising families who contributed to the book by generously and openly sharing their philanthropic stories with us, resulting in the case studies at the end of each section. We would specifically like to thank Maria Ahlström-Bondestam, Sumitra Aswani, Manuel Jose Carvajal, Sara Ojjeh and her sister Lia Ojjeh Martin, Thierry Mauvernay and Cédric Mauvernay, Kristian Parker, Marianne Ruggieri, Ahu Serter and Dr Mary Ann Tsao, who we had the pleasure to work with to learn about their families' philanthropic work.

Thank you to various actors from the Family Business Network, who have been very supportive of the project from the beginning. We would like to thank Alexis Du Roy de Blicquy, Farhad Forbes as well as all the chapter directors who helped us reach out to over 70 families in their global network for the interviews that we conducted in order to better understand philanthropic identities and patterns.

We are very grateful to the team at WISE philanthropy advisors and, especially, to Maurice Machenbaum, Martial Paris and Mael Steiner, for guiding us with practical advice on family philanthropy based on their experience and pioneering approach towards philanthropy. Bruno Auer and Philippe Depoorter were also very supportive during the entire project.

Special thanks also go to IMD and a number of individuals and departments. First of all, we would like to thank Jean-François Manzoni, the President of IMD, for his continuous support and endorsement of all the multiple Chair activities and, in particular, this book project. We are also greatly indebted to Anand Narasimhan who, in his capacity as advisory board member of the Debiopharm Chair as well as Faculty Dean of IMD, has been incredibly supportive of this project. Moreover, the entire team at the Global Family Business Center, namely Matthew Crudgington, Virginie Boillat-Carrard and Lise Moller. Last but not least, this book and the publicity work around it wouldn't have been possible without the great help of our editorial and the communications teams.

Our work is building on that of many outstanding and highly committed thought leaders, of whom we would like to mention a few. Special thanks go to Sharna Goldseker and 21/64 for their great work in the development of tools and frameworks for philanthropists. We would also like to thank Dr John Davis, from the Cambridge Family Enterprise Group, for his pioneering work in the field of family enterprises and the holistic view of the family enterprise system. Lastly, we are grateful to the Philanthropic Initiative in Boston for their work on how to engage the next generation of philanthropists.

Over the course of the last years, earlier versions of the *Family Philanthropy Navigator* were presented and tested in smaller workshops with numerous philanthropists and next generation donors. They deserve our gratitude for sharing their time and experiences with us.

Finally, this book has been shaped by the knowledge and experience of the many individuals and organizations that we have had the privilege of working with over the past decades.

This book has been a collective effort, involving many different types of stakeholders. That is the spirit of the *Family Philanthropy Navigator* and the ideas we actually propose throughout the book – to build a strong ecosystem of partners around you in order to tackle some of the world's greatest societal and environmental challenges. Sharing and exchanging with others, creating and learning together, is a mindset and a way of working, which we very much embrace and encourage. With that, we wish you a great journey!

Peter   Etienne   Malgorzata

MEET THE CREW

Peter Vogel

"To my three children, Sophie, Nina and Alex, who will hopefully have a bright future ahead of them."

The mission of the Debiopharm Chair for Family Philanthropy at IMD is to help aspiring and established philanthropic families start or improve their giving – in a way that is structured, organized, efficient and effective as an integral part of their family enterprise system.

My hope is that this book will challenge, educate and inspire families in their philanthropic activities – whether you are new to giving or have decades of experience. In our workshops, while developing the *Family Philanthropy Navigator*, for example, I have been delighted to see well-established philanthropists finding fresh insight from, and enjoyment in, the toolkit.

Ultimately, I want to see the navigator taking on a life of its own as a tool that families all over the world can find value in as they seek to make a real difference through their giving.

Etienne Eichenberger

"With gratitude to those who love me; with confidence in those who will follow us."

My experience as Co-Founder of WISE philanthropy advisors has shown me that, when well organized, philanthropy can play its part in building innovative and sustainable solutions for local or global challenges. But giving can also become an incredibly rewarding journey for families to engage across generation.

Philanthropy is often an inner journey before it becomes a structured process, as the *Family Philanthropy Navigator* is intended to be for you. The navigator is not about promoting one-size-fits-all, but rather it offers eight important questions for you to address.

My wish is that this book will be an invitation to have meaningful conversations within families so that everyone can be empowered to give more, better and smarter.

Alfredo Carlo, Marcello Petruzzi and Beatrice Schena

Our design studio Housatonic exists to facilitate communication among people and we strongly believe that design, when well done, can help organizations and our communities to be more inclusive and sustainable, just like philanthropy.

This project is the demonstration that philanthropy is not something for the few but an aspiration for the many, and that we can all contribute to a better world in different ways and at many levels.

Our hope is that the *Family Philanthropy Navigator* will make conversations better, and even more profound, around a topic that is relevant for every one of us and key in designing a better future for our planet.

Małgorzata Kurak

"To my parents for all of their love and support. They have been a source of motivation and inspiration all these years."

Giving is complex, and it can become even more complex when you are giving together with your own family.

My contribution to the field of family philanthropy comes through my research at the Debiopharm Chair for Family Philanthropy, through which I've had the pleasure to meet so many good-hearted (business) people who have generously shared their philanthropic stories with us – their successes, but also their failures. We are greatly indebted to all of these enterprising families who have participated in our research project, for supporting us, but also for their courage in doing good where it is most needed. Their support and feedback while developing the navigator has shown us that this tool is truly needed, now more than ever.

My sincere hope is that the navigator will ignite philanthropy in each of us, and in each of our families.

Matt Falloon

Partnership is vital in philanthropy, and it has been just as important in the unique creation of this book. From different viewpoints and experiences, we galvanized quickly as a close-knit team around a shared purpose. Many paths and ideas were considered, but we found our way forward by working together to challenge and encourage one another.

I hope you will sense this spirit of partnership throughout this book and be inspired by it. After all, effective family philanthropy means learning to work with diverse partners in a spirit of equality, respect and solidarity so that everyone can reach their destination.

FOREWORD

Thierry Mauvernay, Chairman of Debiopharm

Philanthropy and Social Impact

A few years ago, after offering US$10,000 from her own pocket, a famous actress managed to raise $1 million from business people. This donation made it possible to give Tanzania 350,000 free mosquito nets, a well-known way of combating malaria, which is a scourge in that country. In reality, however, the nets have instead often been used to make wedding dresses. In addition, local shopkeepers complained that this aid destabilized the local economic network. As one daily newspaper reported, development aid professionals also questioned the effectiveness of this one-off action, preferring a voucher distribution program offering an 80% to 90% discount on the purchase of mosquito nets. The latter requires a contribution from very poor people, but it has a lasting impact because, in African culture, what is free has no value.

The initial idea was good. But when it comes to philanthropy, a traveler's backpack and good intentions are not enough. You can't just improvise yourself as a donor. Giving in an effective way is not as simple as it seems. Spontaneous giving often does not achieve the expected results or reach the right people. Unfortunately, this has often been the case in recent disasters.

Managing Donations Effectively

Philanthropy requires rigorous and professional management, even if the desire to help others often stems from emotion. It's important to feel passionate about a cause. It allows you to get involved in a project, but it is not enough to create a positive and lasting impact on the lives of the beneficiaries. It is imperative to know how to surround yourself with experts who master the constraints of the field and the local cultural particularities.

Family companies, which represent more than 70% of the world's businesses, thus make a major contribution to today's global economy and philanthropy. It is for this reason that we have created the Debiopharm Chair for Family Philanthropy at IMD in Lausanne, with the aim of increasing the social and financial impact of donor families. This Chair aims to develop the field of knowledge in family philanthropy, to disseminate best practices and to provide donors with tools to strengthen analysis, decision-making processes, performance indicators and governance.

A professional approach to philanthropy consists of making optimal use of necessarily limited resources. This is the very definition of good management. Resources will always fall far below what is needed and rigorously managing available grants and resources is vital. In Vietnam, for example, thanks to loans of $50 to $150, the income of thousands of families has risen in three to four years from 50 cents a day per person – at that point you are in basic survival mode – to more than a dollar a day – at which point, you move to a more stable existence. This difference may seem small, but for these people it changes everything. A well-conducted philanthropic action also makes it possible to create leverage effects, for example, to mobilize public funding, which multiplies the impact of private aid. In some countries, there are funding programs whereby when a dollar is given, the state invests the same amount.

The Donation Also Benefits the Donor

The donation can also benefit the donor. Very often, in a family, money does not bring people together – it divides them. The passing of time does not unite either, it separates the generations. What unites people are values. Today, in companies, employees generally want to give purpose to their work. When they look for a job, for example, they find out about their future employer, its activities and its values as well. Debiopharm has 41 nationalities among its employees, who come from a variety of backgrounds. They have different cultures and ages. How do you bring them together around a project? I like to say that we are all similar, but not identical. What will bring us together is to share the same values. A company should no longer just be judged on its financial performance, but also on its positive impact. Family philanthropy should make it possible to unite both family members and company staff around common values.

This is why the second aim of this Chair is to consider philanthropy as a catalyst for the transmission of values within the company and between the different generations. Philanthropy can become a management tool that strengthens ties through shared values, thus contributing to continuity. As André Malraux predicted, the 21st century will either be spiritual or not. For me, spirituality and values are very complementary notions. In the future there will be a limit to materialism. We must also give meaning to our actions. Philanthropy can provide this meaning. We must do everything we can to encourage it.

The *Family Philanthropy Navigator* is an important and timely contribution to the evolving needs and role of philanthropy in the world at large and within the family enterprise system. In line with the mission of the Philanthropy Chair at IMD, it helps families of all sizes and backgrounds understand, professionalize and optimize their giving through simple, practical tools and expert guidance from leading academics and practitioners in the field. I sincerely hope that it will be widely used by families around the world, seeing it as a source of inspiration, a trigger for initiating or improving conversations amongst family members and, ultimately, a catalyst to improve the state of the world through family philanthropy.

Get Ready for Your Philanthropic Journey

2 **The Need for a Family Philanthropy Navigator**

12 **Introducing The Navigator**

1

Get Ready for Your Philanthropic Journey

The Need for a Family Philanthropy Navigator

Welcome to the *Family Philanthropy Navigator* – your personal guide to a rewarding and impactful journey in giving as an aspiring or experienced philanthropist.

Are you a budding philanthropist who dreams of making a positive impact in the world? Are you an experienced philanthropist keen to finetune your family's giving? Are you an established philanthropic family that wants to press the reset button and take a different approach?

If so, the *Family Philanthropy Navigator* is for you.

Through the *Family Philanthropy Navigator*, our intention is simple: to provide a one-stop, practical and interactive, step-by-step pathway that can be used by any novice or experienced philanthropist to begin or improve their journeys in giving, no matter what their circumstances, resources or ambitions might be.

You may ask, why a navigator? Well, philanthropy is not just an expression of blind faith or a simple gesture of generosity. Your giving might well begin with an inspiring vision to change the world or with one act of kindness, but very soon it becomes a journey, just like a journey at sea; and as for any successful journey, you require a precise understanding of where you are, where you want to go and what the best way is to get there. The person that is typically in charge of this task on a ship is the "navigator." We have therefore selected the metaphor of a ship that sets out on a grand voyage into uncharted territory.

It is worth remembering that there are many ways for a boat to reach a harbor and, indeed, there are many harbors and many boats. In philanthropy, there is no one-size-fits-all guarantee of safe passage, either. The important thing is to choose goals and chart the course that best suits you and your family. Success in philanthropy means different things to different people, and it depends on individual circumstances and preferences.

We believe that there are no specific "right" or "wrong" approaches to philanthropy, and that any journey in giving will have wins and losses that we can learn from and share. While there are just as many ways to approach philanthropy, if approached in a thoughtful and structured way, family giving can be an impactful and engaging calling. It can become a lifelong passion as you start to see that you can make a difference in the world.

For many aspiring and established philanthropists, the perennial question is how to successfully navigate the world of philanthropy and achieve your aims. How will you choose and then reach your destination? How long will it take? What do you need to complete the journey? How can you mobilize your resources as well as your personal and professional network, in order to become more effective? What happens if you stray off course?

Philanthropy can serve multiple purposes. Philanthropy, first and foremost, means to give personal resources to public benefit.

However, we believe that it can also have great fringe benefits for the family itself. For many families, it has become an integral part of the family enterprise system and a vehicle to ensure family unity and engagement across the generations.

Trying to balance these multiple purposes simultaneously requires careful navigation and guidance. Having seen the many twists and turns faced by new and experienced philanthropic families, we created this book and practical tool to make your journey through the world of giving as clear, enjoyable and impactful as possible.

Each family is unique and every journey in giving is unique, but there are tried and tested ways, centuries of know-how and a growing body of expert insight and advice that can help to guide you as you embark on your journey.

In writing this book, we have drawn on decades of shared experience working with philanthropists from all over the world – witnessing their unique challenges,

The Need for a Family Philanthropy Navigator

Get Ready for Your Philanthropic Journey

exploring best practices and trends, sharing successes and struggles, and helping families of all shapes and sizes make a real difference.

It could be funding advocacy on climate change, investing in vaccines for new epidemics, supporting a university, donating to a museum or supporting the education of underserved communities in far flung places; philanthropy is a big tent that has room and opportunity for all enterprising families, no matter what their interests, resources or ambitions.

Engaging in a sustainable course of giving involves many more hurdles than often anticipated. From managing family dynamics and building healthy partnerships to choosing the right governance structures and measuring impact, philanthropy can soon become an exciting adventure – much like a voyage across an ocean.

Even the most experienced sailors can run aground or veer off course. The *Family Philanthropy Navigator* seeks to provide a steady hand on the rudder for philanthropists of all kinds through the swells, lulls and storms so that you can pilot your ship successfully towards its destination.

Before we get started, let's set the scene. Why is philanthropy so important in today's world and why is it important that philanthropists think about how they can make their giving more effective and efficient?

A Changing World and the Growing Importance of Philanthropy

Leaders around the world are confronted with major challenges, many of which seem too big to be resolved by a single set of stakeholders alone. The Fourth Industrial Revolution is disrupting the way we live and work, forcing us to rethink our strategies and core beliefs.

Further, the world is facing major challenges on a societal and environmental level, as summarized in the United Nations Sustainable Development Goals (UN SDGs) 2030. There is a rapidly growing gap between rich and poor, continued inequality and poverty in many places, an unresolved youth unemployment crisis around the world, as well as increasing demographic pressure due to a growing and aging population. The economic growth and expansion of the past decades is catching up with us and threatening to irreversibly change our ocean, air and land systems, which are approaching critical tipping points, as illustrated in the symbolic Earth Overshoot Day, which marks the date when humanity's demand for ecological resources and services in a given year exceeds what Earth can regenerate in that year.

Never before have leaders been so uncertain about the answers to these questions and challenges. However, these issues require immediate attention from public policy, businesses and broader society. The social contract between different stakeholders is changing and is forcing all of us to rethink our position on these matters and our role in the economy and society. Yet, it is anything but easy to resolve these challenges because there is no one-size-fits-all solution. Instead, collective action and an interplay between stakeholders is required – including public policy, businesses, non-governmental organizations (NGOs), affluent families and philanthropists, and the broader public. In this mix of stakeholders, enterprising families have long played a role in tackling societal and environmental challenges.

Over the past decades and centuries, philanthropy has come a long way. Just like the world around us, philanthropy is in constant flux. It is a living and breathing phenomenon that has evolved over time as societies – and families – have changed. We would like to take a few moments to guide you through the ever-changing map of philanthropy to illustrate some of the most important trends that are shaping the practice of organized giving today.

While today's word philanthropy originates from Greek, the concept of charitable giving has long been present in almost all cultures and religions around the world. Since those early days, philanthropy – the desire to promote the welfare of others through the donation of resources to good causes – has established itself as an influential and very well-organized force for good. Many enterprising families around the world are philanthropically active, whether sharing wealth from the success of a family business or donating time and skills to support others. Philanthropy provides a meaningful way to drive positive change and to promote family values and unity.

Philanthropy's growth around the globe has been far from homogenous, with many variations sprouting up in different cultures and ages. However, in broad terms, we observe three major waves of philanthropy that illustrate the general evolution of giving.

The Three Waves of Philanthropy

The concept and word "philanthropy" was coined 2,500 years ago in the Ancient Greek tragedy *Prometheus Bound*, in which Prometheus is punished for defying Zeus by helping humanity through the gifts of fire, hope, art and sciences.
In the play, Prometheus is described as having a humanity-loving character – *philanthropos tropos*. This idea of wanting to help others, even if there is a price, has remained steadfast as the keystone value of philanthropy as it has emerged and developed in more recent centuries.

The Need for a Family Philanthropy Navigator

Get Ready for Your Philanthropic Journey

These waves can help us to understand the ongoing transformation of philanthropy and what is influencing the field of family philanthropy today.

FIRST WAVE OF PHILANTHROPY

THE WORD ORIGINATES FROM GREEK (PHILANTHROPOS)

CHARITY MAINLY THROUGH RELIGIOUS STRUCTURES

BEFORE MID 18th CENTURY

SECOND WAVE OF PHILANTHROPY

UPPER CLASSES AND NEWLY AFFLUENT INDIVIDUALS

↓

MAXIMIZING THE UTILITY OF GRANT MAKING THROUGH A STRUCTURED APPROACH

(COMBINE, INSTITUTIONALIZE FOCUS AND ORGANIZE THE EFFORTS)

DURING 18th–19th CENTURY

THIRD WAVE OF PHILANTHROPY

MAJOR TRANSFORMATION

- DIGITAL TECHNOLOGY
- HYPER SUCCESSFUL ENTREPRENEURS
- NEED TO WORK IN COMPLEMENT WITH OTHER STAKEHOLDERS

↓

DIFFERENT APPROACH TO GIVING

TODAY

Family Philanthropy Navigator

The First Wave of Philanthropy

The first wave of philanthropy spans the many centuries before the mid-18th century. During that time, charity was mainly conducted through religious structures. Most religions have incorporated elements of charitable giving and have promoted forms of organized giving, such as "tithing," to support those less fortunate.

From alms-giving, handouts from monarchs to the collective charitable traditions of organized religion, this wave lay the foundations for the future of philanthropy, building on the concept of sharing wealth in any form or size out of a spirit of benevolence, civic duty or the idea that you become a better person as you give.

The Second Wave of Philanthropy

The second wave of philanthropy emerged in the 18th and 19th centuries as the upper classes and newly affluent individuals and families sought to combine, institutionalize, focus and organize the way they shared their wealth to achieve benefits for society through charitable giving. The central idea was to maximize the utility of grant making.

One of the earliest examples of a charitable foundation can be found in London in the Age of Enlightenment. The Foundling Hospital was a pioneering facility founded by sea captain Thomas Coram in 1739 to educate, support and house destitute and poor children. The institution even had a Royal Charter that set out its governing principles and goals as well as an array of guardians and governors, drawn from 18th-century aristocracy and nobility.

From these early examples of organized philanthropy, the practice flourished as the Industrial Revolution transformed the fortunes of many economies and families. George Peabody, who is the acknowledged father of modern philanthropy, started to endow libraries and museums in the United States and fund housing for poor people in London in the 1860s. His approach to giving served as the model for Andrew Carnegie, John D. Rockefeller and many others.

The Third Wave of Philanthropy

In recent decades, philanthropy has been undergoing another major transformation, in part due to innovations in digital technology, the rise of a new wave of hyper successful entrepreneurs and the need to work together with other stakeholders who have different approaches to giving.

This wave has been characterized and shaped by certain trends that differ from the activities of traditional philanthropists.

Get Ready for Your Philanthropic Journey

THE NINE TRENDS OF MODERN PHILANTHROPY

1. INCLUSIVENESS OF GIVING

Driven by advances in technology, giving has become highly democratized. First, mass collaboration allows everyone to make a contribution to the greater good of society. Second, online philanthropy marketplaces allow everyone to contribute to specific causes, even with just a few dollars. Third, aggregated funds are forming, combining the resources of many donors in the most effective ways.

2. NEXT GENERATION AS AGENTS OF CHANGE

We are in the middle of one of the greatest transfers of wealth in human history, with the next generation (largely Millennials and digital natives) taking over the reins and moving into powerful positions within their families. They come in with a fresh mindset, new ideas and they feel a great sense of responsibility to become agents of change.

3. REAL-TIME GLOBAL AWARENESS

Improved access to the Internet has placed a greater and more detailed spotlight on many more needs and causes around the world, raising awareness and making them more visible to donors. It has also made it easier to connect donors with causes and organizations around the world, so that solutions can be found.

4. SPENDING DOWN

Many philanthropists are choosing to spend down their funds instead of, for example, donating the interest from perpetual funds. They prefer to give while they are alive instead of trying to create a legacy after they pass away.

Family Philanthropy Navigator

5. RISE OF MEGA-DONORS

In recent decades, we have observed the rise of a new breed of mega-donors – individuals who have accumulated their wealth in a matter of years rather than generations and who have decided to use (part of) that wealth to do good in the world. The likes of George Soros, Bill Gates and Mark Zuckerberg have led the charge, seeking to control how they give back in specific ways.

6. RISE OF MULTI-STAKEHOLDER EFFORTS

In this new "era of impact," we can observe a convergence of the different stakeholder groups, including traditional charities and philanthropists, businesses and investors, as well as policy-makers. They are collectively striving towards impact.

7. RISE OF EFFECTIVE and IMPACT-DRIVEN GIVING

There is a clear shift towards measurable and sustainable impact of philanthropic giving. Donors are demanding clear key performance indicators (KPIs) – which is evidently easier for some projects and more difficult for others – to ensure that their money is being put to use in an effective and efficient manner.

8. FOCUS ON ISSUES RATHER THAN PLACES

In the time of the UN SDGs 2030, philanthropy has become more and more focused on specific issues and causes rather than places. Philanthropists are often acting more globally than locally.

9. RISE OF COHESIVE GIVING

Families have embraced a more cohesive approach to philanthropy by aligning their giving closely with their business activities as part of an overarching approach inspired by a sense of higher purpose and social value creation.

Get Ready for Your Philanthropic Journey

As a consequence of these trends, philanthropy is becoming more organized, transparent and professionalized as more families seek to achieve sustainable, measurable impact in an efficient manner through building effective partnerships at all levels of the giving ecosystem. Over the coming years, these trends will further gain in importance and continue to transform the field of family philanthropy.

Philanthropy and the Family

As the changing face of philanthropy has ebbed and flowed through the ages, enterprising families have also adapted to the times to meet their own needs and the demands of the local or global economy. In tandem, the role of giving within families has undergone a similar process of evolution.

In fact, philanthropy is no longer regarded as just a separate vehicle for enterprising families to "do good." The most effective philanthropic families appreciate that philanthropy is best treated as an integral part of the family enterprise system, including their business(es), family office and other investment activities, family- and ownership-related activities as well as their philanthropic and social impact activities.[1]

Understanding the full scope of what they do and how those elements are interconnected enables families to grow stronger together cohesively and to achieve multi-generational success.

In fact, far from serving as an outlier or afterthought, philanthropy now plays a critical role for enterprising families. To paraphrase the late US President, John F. Kennedy, the question has become not just about what families do in philanthropy but about what philanthropy can do for the family. Yes, philanthropic families perform a crucial duty in helping to tackle the world's challenges, but philanthropy also serves an intrinsic and positive purpose within the family unit.

Philanthropy can provide a relatively neutral space for families to develop a shared understanding and spark conversations and joint experiences across generations, while doing good.

Philanthropy helps in educating family members in skills or behaviors that are important in the sustainability and longevity of the family system, such as the concept of family legacy, caring for each other, financial literacy or project management and the idea of the responsibility that comes with wealth.

10   Family Philanthropy Navigator

Philanthropy can be leveraged as a vehicle for inclusiveness by empowering family members who may not be actively involved in the family business to make a meaningful contribution to the family enterprise with their own talents.

Philanthropy can provide an opportunity for generations to meet around common goals. It might help to onboard the next generation into the family enterprise and help the elder generation to better understand the fresh perspectives of the younger generation.

Giving builds up valuable social and reputational capital for families and demonstrates their long-term commitment to the health and stability of society – a crucial factor for all families. It can also inspire greater loyalty among employees and create a higher sense of purpose.

Philanthropy and its role within families have come a long way from humble beginnings. Not only is philanthropy becoming more professional and organized in an ever-complex environment but its importance for the long-term success and unity of families is growing.

With this in mind, the *Family Philanthropy Navigator* was conceived, triggered by the demand for easy-to-use but comprehensive toolkits and guidance for aspiring and experienced philanthropic families around the world to make the most of their giving.

---

1. The term "family enterprise system" was coined by John Davis in 2013.

Get Ready for Your Philanthropic Journey

Introducing the Navigator

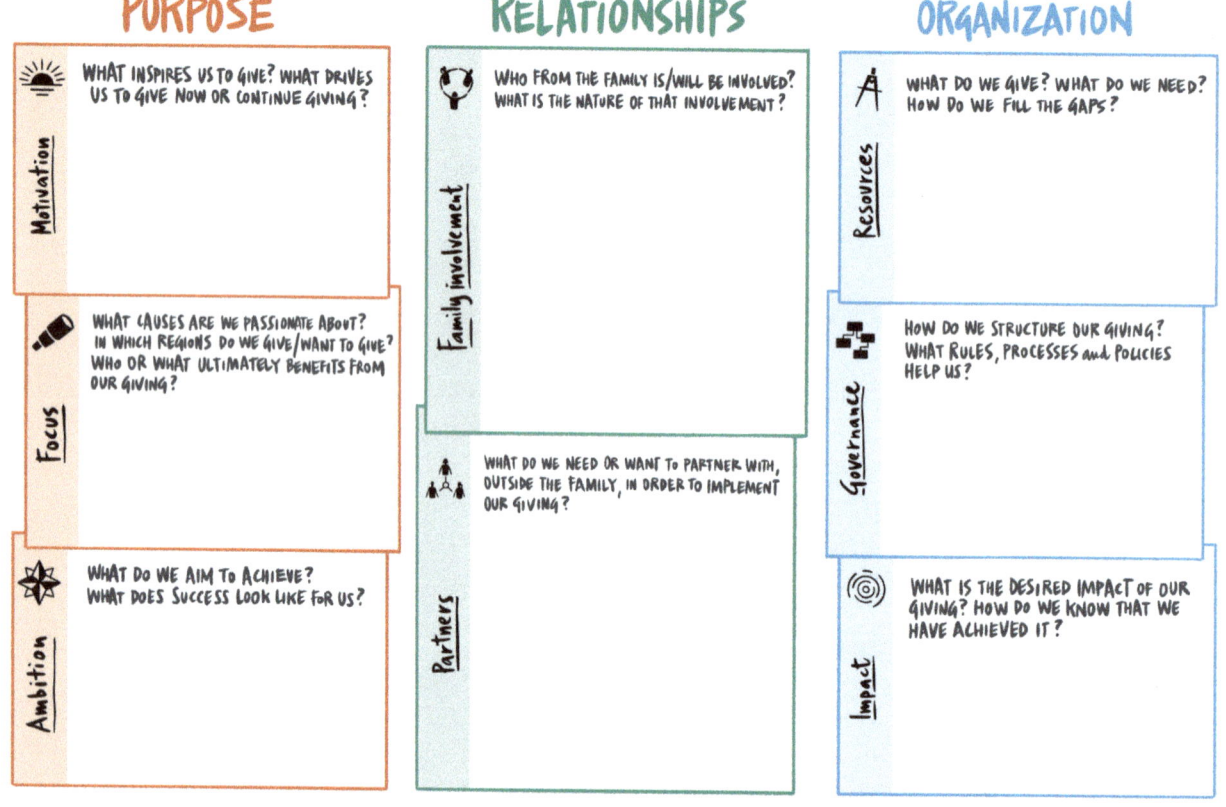

12 Family Philanthropy Navigator

Over the past years and decades, we have had the pleasure to work with many inspiring enterprising and philanthropic families from around the world – as academics, advisors and practitioners.

We came to realize that many of the fundamental challenges and questions are mostly the same across families and felt that if we could lay these out in a logical structure, it might be of great value to families who are seeking advice or guidance in their giving journey.

In late 2017, we put together an early prototype of the navigator and started using it extensively in our training, workshops, research projects and advisory work. Families have responded very positively to the types of discussions that the tool and related activities have triggered, which ultimately led us to start working on this book.

The *Family Philanthropy Navigator* is a hands-on guide for novice and experienced philanthropists and their families. It is a practical and engaging tool that will enable families to get together to answer the core questions at the heart of any voyage in giving: why, what, who and how?

The *Family Philanthropy Navigator* is comprised of core sections and eight building blocks:

→ **PURPOSE** of your giving, including your **motivation**, **focus** and **ambition**.

→ **RELATIONSHIPS** you need to activate your giving, including **family involvement** and **partners**.

→ **ORGANIZATION** of your giving, including **resources**, **governance** and **impact**.

→ A dedicated chapter on **LEARNING**, providing you with a framework to continuously review, assess and improve your giving.

Introducing the Navigator

Get Ready for Your Philanthropic Journey

WHY and WHAT
The first pillar of the *Family Philanthropy Navigator* is the Purpose of your giving.
It includes your motivation to be philanthropically active, explores what you wish to focus on in your giving and your ambition and goals.

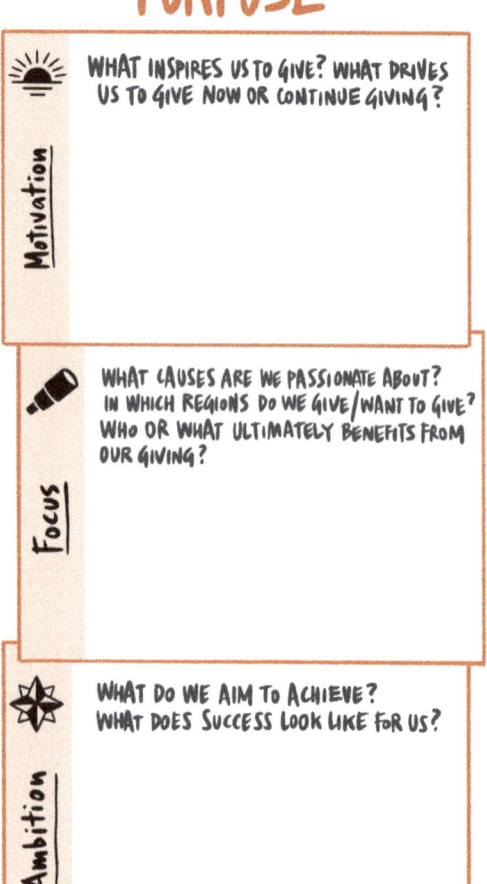

WHO and WITH WHOM
The second pillar of the *Family Philanthropy Navigator* focuses on the Relationships of your giving. It explores who from your family and a wider partner ecosystem should get involved in your journey and how they can make a meaningful contribution to the long-term success of your giving.

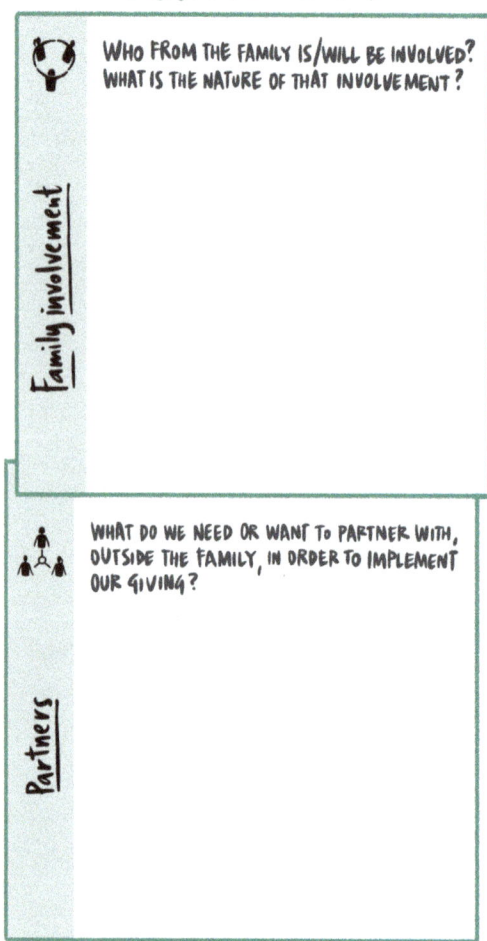

PURPOSE

Motivation — WHAT INSPIRES US TO GIVE? WHAT DRIVES US TO GIVE NOW OR CONTINUE GIVING?

Focus — WHAT CAUSES ARE WE PASSIONATE ABOUT? IN WHICH REGIONS DO WE GIVE/WANT TO GIVE? WHO OR WHAT ULTIMATELY BENEFITS FROM OUR GIVING?

Ambition — WHAT DO WE AIM TO ACHIEVE? WHAT DOES SUCCESS LOOK LIKE FOR US?

RELATIONSHIPS

Family involvement — WHO FROM THE FAMILY IS/WILL BE INVOLVED? WHAT IS THE NATURE OF THAT INVOLVEMENT?

Partners — WHAT DO WE NEED OR WANT TO PARTNER WITH, OUTSIDE THE FAMILY, IN ORDER TO IMPLEMENT OUR GIVING?

HOW
The third pillar of the *Family Philanthropy Navigator* focuses on the Organization of your giving. It focuses on some of the core structural elements of your giving journey including resources, the governance mechanisms as well as your approach to ensuring that your giving has a lasting positive impact.

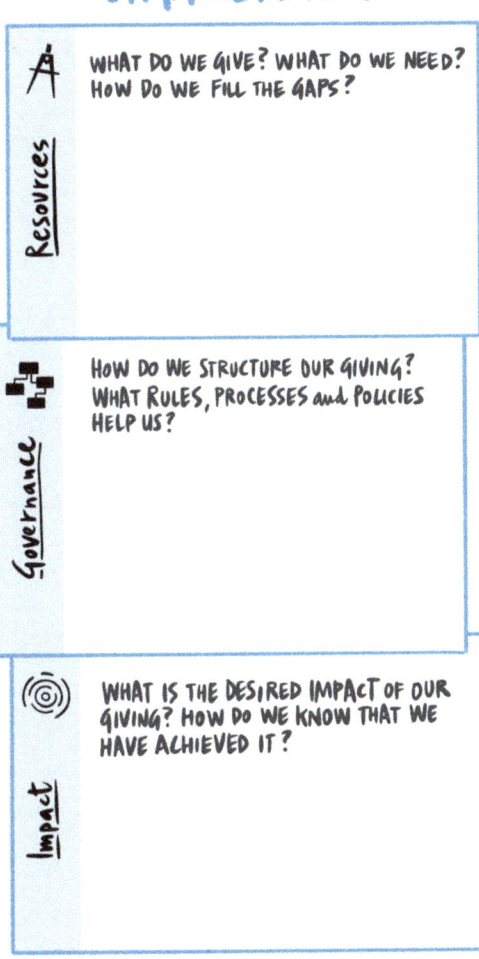

Introducing the Navigator 15

Get Ready for Your Philanthropic Journey

How to Use the Navigator

There are, of course, no "set in stone" rules as to how you should be using the *Family Philanthropy Navigator*, but there are two approaches we recommend:

1. You can move through each chapter in a step-by-step approach from start to finish. This could prove most rewarding for novice philanthropists who are just getting started on their giving journey or for experienced philanthropists who are looking to reassess their giving holistically.
2. You can use the navigator as an inspirational guide if you are seeking insight on a specific aspect of your giving. In that case, you can jump to the respective chapter in the book. This approach would be useful for experienced philanthropists looking to assess and enhance specific areas of their giving. It is advisable, however, to then ensure that whatever changes you might make to your giving are still aligned with the overall approach.

Structure of the Building Blocks

The building blocks of the *Family Philanthropy Navigator* are described in separate chapters of the book which all follow the same structure, including an introduction, a number of critical trade-offs and decisions you will need to make, and some practical activities for you and your family. Moreover, each section concludes with inspiring case studies from around the world.

Setting the Compass (Trade-Offs)

As part of a joint research project with the Family Business Network (FBN), we have conducted in-depth interviews with nearly 100 philanthropic families from around the world. We realized that there are almost as many philanthropic identities and patterns as there are philanthropists. We would receive a multitude of answers to the same question, which ultimately led us to integrate a total of 32 trade-offs into the book. These are designed to help you make important decisions with respect to your philanthropic journey.

On the next page, you can see one example of such a trade-off as it is featured in the book.

Often, these trade-offs are presented as a spectrum with two opposing views and many hybrid solutions in between. Selected questions can help you and your family identify where you stand on the spectrum. Different family members will likely have a range of views with respect to where they would like to position your family's philanthropic efforts. This will yield important conversations amongst the family. We recommend that you set aside time to consider each of these trade-offs, both individually and as a family.

UNILATERAL ⟷ COLLABORATIVE

Giving solely

Giving in collaboration with others

"If you want to go quickly, go alone. If you want to go far, go together." In philanthropy, you can work on your own or in multiple combinations with others. Given that a foundation does not have shareholders, "clients" or an owner, a foundation enjoys a unique freedom to act. Decide whether you would prefer the quick decision making and autonomy of flying solo, or whether you would prefer to include other donors or foundations in your philanthropic journey. Collaboration can lead to new ideas, new networks and this can lead to better results, but it also requires greater coordination.

→ Do you want to go it **alone** in your giving? If not, how **collaborative** do you want to be with others such as **foundations** or **other partners**?
→ How much **freedom** do you want in your giving?
→ How does this **relate** to the **focus** and **ambitions** of your philanthropy?

Get Ready for Your Philanthropic Journey

Activities

The activities in this book have been prepared as simple, useful and practical exercises to inform your decisions. Each activity will enable you to gain clarity and test your choices as you move towards answering the key navigator questions.

We highly recommend that you take the opportunity to engage with family members by using these activities as a catalyst and platform for transparent discussion and co-creation.

It is worth noting that some activities are interconnected across different parts of the navigator because those topics share common ground and should be considered in tandem, such as Activity 2 of **Family Involvement**, Activity 2 of **Partners** and Activity 2 of **Resources**.

Insights

Throughout the book, you will see orange boxes within chapters that are tagged as **Insight**. These boxes contain specific tips, guidance and advice or flag up challenges that are associated with the relevant subject areas.

We suggest that you pause, read and reflect on each of these boxes as you work through the book, regardless of whether you are novice or experienced in philanthropy.

The information they contain will certainly prove valuable at some point in your journey, whether that means helping you strengthen your approach, prepare for or overcome a challenge, or avoid a mishap along the way.

Case Studies

The case studies have been selected with care to provide helpful examples of diverse enterprising families at different stages in their philanthropy. We have chosen them because we felt that each of them can serve as a source of inspiration for you as you are developing your own giving journey.

Each section of the navigator has three case studies. Besides providing some background information about the family and their philanthropy, the nine case studies feature the families' answers to the corresponding navigator questions, providing you with examples of how certain trade-offs and dilemmas relate to their experience. Moreover, the families have shared their personal learnings and recommendations.

Introducing the Navigator

[Get Ready for Your Philanthropic Journey](#)

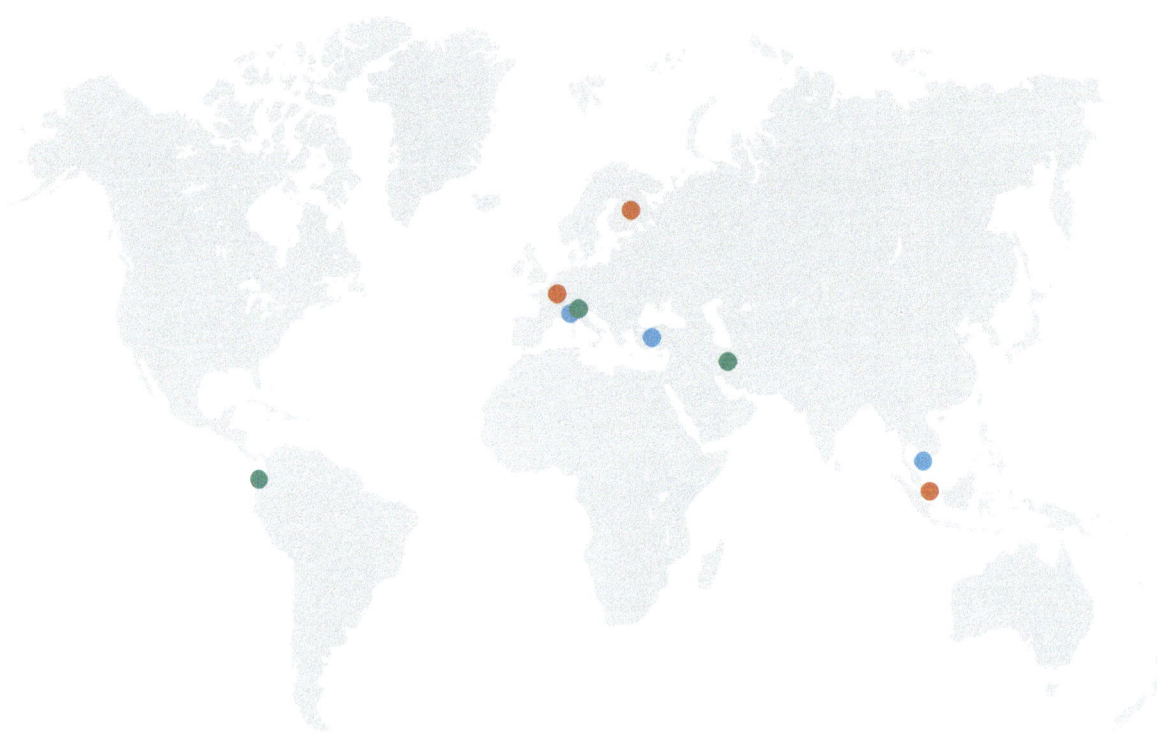

Case Studies

PURPOSE

Eva Ahlström Foundation
Maria Ahlström-Bondestam

Tsao Ng Yu Shun Foundation
Dr Mary Ann Tsao

Fondation Juniclair
Marianne Ruggeri

RELATIONSHIPS

Bloom Fund
Sarah Ojjeh and Lia Ojjeh Martin

Oak Foundation
Kristian Parker

Carvajal Foundation
Manuel Jose Carvajal

ORGANIZATION

Fark Holding
Ahu Büyükkuşoğlu Serter

Fondation Philanthropique Next
Thierry and Cédric Mauvernay

Ishk Tolaram Foundation
Sumitra Aswani

Learning

Integrating learning into your giving journey is critical because the world around us is in constant flux. What might be true today might no longer be true tomorrow. Giving is a dynamic process and over time, our beliefs, knowledge, experience and interests might change, which is why it is important to regularly review and adjust your assumptions. Given its importance, and because it relates to all areas of the *Family Philanthropy Navigator*, we have created a separate section dedicated to learning.

This section will help you and your family renew and upgrade your approach to philanthropy across all eight building blocks. We recommend that you return to these exercises regularly as you progress in your philanthropic activities, both individually and collectively, to take stock and make any necessary changes. An inventory of assessment questions will help you initiate your learning process.

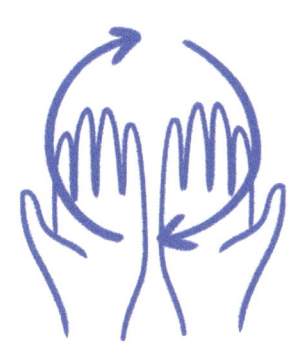

Hoisting Sail, Together

The navigator was built as an accessible and easy-to-use platform for families to discuss and agree on ways to launch or improve their philanthropy. Indeed, the tool and its activities can be printed out or projected onto a screen as working boards to encourage interaction and creativity.

By coming together and collaborating through the navigator, families can move towards the common understanding, delicate compromises, joint solutions and key decisions that are required for any successful philanthropic endeavor.

We hope that your encounter with the navigator will prove enriching and enjoyable as a family activity, nurturing closer bonds and deeper understanding, while also creating shared memories and moments.

It might be that, somewhere within the process of completing the navigator, you come to realize that you have some questions, are stuck, or simply might need some outside advice. This is normal because many of the questions we raise in the book will trigger insightful, yet sometimes also challenging, discussions amongst family members. Feel free to reach out to us anytime and we will try our best to help you negotiate your way through the *Family Philanthropy Navigator*.

So, let's get started. All hands on deck. It's time to set sail with the *Family Philanthropy Navigator*.

Introducing the Navigator

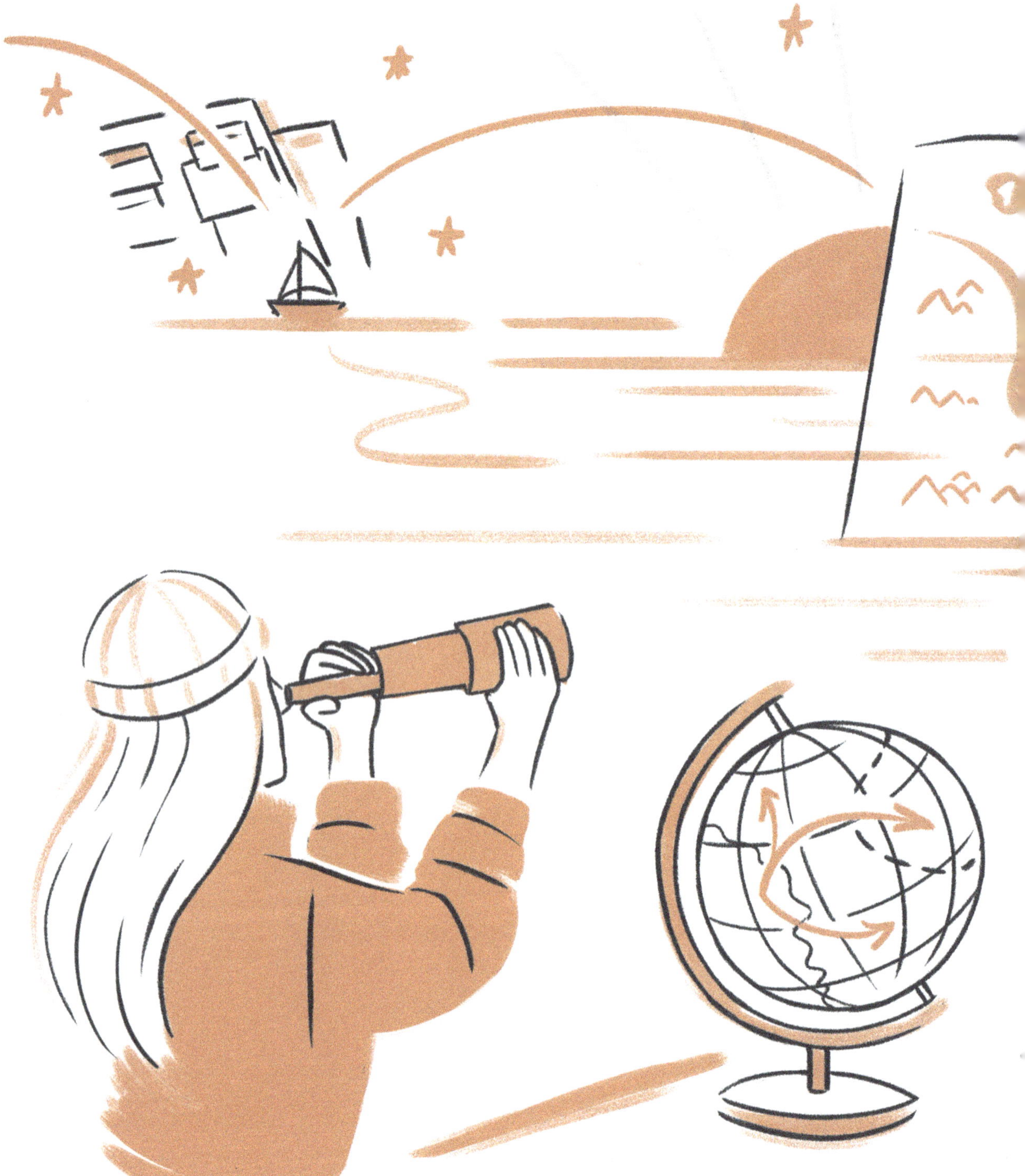

Purpose

30 **Motivation**

42 **Focus**

56 **Ambition**

68 **Case Studies**

Purpose

Introduction

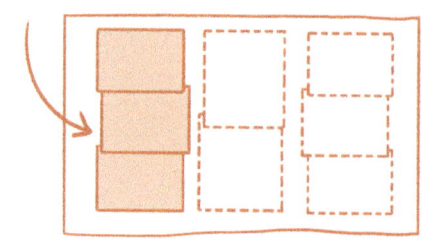

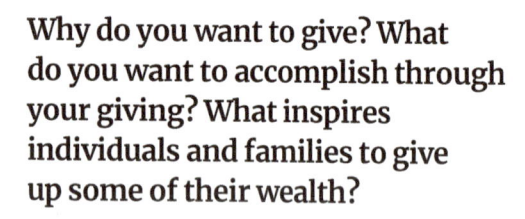

Why do you want to give? What do you want to accomplish through your giving? What inspires individuals and families to give up some of their wealth?

Giving is a deeply personal journey before it becomes a process – it's a unique blend of who we are as human beings, and how we see the world and our place in it. Do you dream of helping to find a cure for cancer, raise awareness in the fight for women's rights, or do you want to restore a museum to its former glory? Would you like to bring your family closer together or pass on important values to the next generation? How do you see your and your family's roles and responsibilities in society?

There are no right or wrong reasons for becoming a philanthropist. For some, giving is a calling. For others, it's inspired by a significant life event such as the loss of a loved one. It might be that you want to correct an injustice that you have seen somewhere in the world – either socially or environmentally.

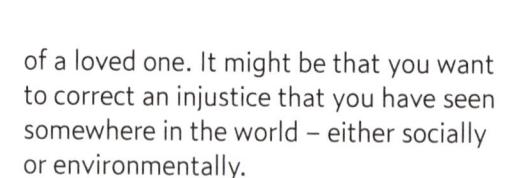

It can, of course, be less emotional: driven by a sense of social obligation, a prudent way to manage wealth, a mechanism to boost the family or business brand, or a backbone of family governance. Philanthropy can be inspired and driven by passion or it can be a pragmatic decision based on tax considerations or financial realities.

PURPOSE is fundamental to the act of giving and the first port of call for our navigator. There are many considerations that you and your family should address when it comes to defining the purpose of your giving. By the end of this section, you will have explored these key themes and have a clear understanding of the purpose that will fuel your philanthropy.

The main navigator questions that you and your family will answer at this stage are:

> → **Motivation**: What is our motivation? What inspires us to give? What drives us to give now or continue giving?
>
> → **Focus**: What is our focus? What causes are we passionate about? In which regions do we give/want to give? Who or what ultimately benefits from our giving?
>
> → **Ambition**: What are our ambitions? What do we aim to achieve? What does success look like for us?

Set aside sufficient time for a period of soul-searching and contemplation. The conclusions you draw and the decisions you make at this stage will inform and shape many steps that will follow. Within the navigator, many of the other dimensions are directly related to and dependent on this first step because giving becomes particularly rewarding, and can be more effective, if your philanthropic actions mirror your purpose, including your fundamental beliefs and values – as an individual or as a family.

So what is **PURPOSE**, and how does it relate to philanthropy? Purpose is the moral compass and sense of determination that informs and drives our decisions and actions. For many people, having a purpose that inspires the way they live and work provides much needed momentum, resilience and a sense of achievement and meaning.

If our goal in philanthropy is effective and impactful giving, then purpose can help improve the journey. Purpose enables us to make informed and relevant decisions in the day-to-day realities and challenges of philanthropy. With purpose, we are able to distinguish between choices that are genuinely worthwhile and appropriate for us, and those that are simply easy or technically correct.

Introduction 25

Purpose

Purpose not only frames and strengthens your philanthropy, it can also help to unite and motivate your family around collective goals and values. With purpose, it is easier to achieve what you set out to do and to build enduring relationships with your partners. It can help you choose appropriate partners with similar values and it gives them better insight to understand where you are coming from.

Clear and well-articulated ambitions, as part of an overarching purpose, will enrich your vision and communication with partners, providing a sense of direction that will inspire and galvanize your philanthropic ecosystem.

On the other hand, philanthropy without purpose can feel destined for disappointment. Why? Well, a lack of a defined or shared purpose often leads to a lack of clarity, poor engagement and weak decision making. Without purpose, it is likely that you will tend to make decisions with only the short term in mind. These can, in turn, result in ill-advised strategies and unintended negative consequences for you, your family and your partners.

When we set off on any kind of journey, it helps to have direction and purpose – otherwise, we are at the mercy of the elements. A well-defined purpose acts like a trusty compass; it shows the way and keeps you on track, even when the going gets tough or the fog obscures the way ahead.

As a family, reflecting on your purpose can be both a challenging but also a fulfilling experience. An open exchange about your philanthropic activities – whether new or established – can be beneficial to the family as you will be learning about similarities and differences in interests and values. Failing to address and find answers for these important questions could create problems further into the journey. Clarity and self-awareness at this early stage will smooth the path forward and inspire stronger decisions, more engagement and better results.

Embedding philanthropy within the wider family enterprise system can become a unique opportunity to share knowledge across generations, foster inter-generational collaboration, and empower the next generation. It also offers otherwise less-engaged family members a chance to contribute in a meaningful way, even though they might not be active in the business.

Insight

THINK FAMILY

The purpose behind your giving is complex and personal but, if you hope to engage with and include family members during your philanthropic journey, it is advisable to discuss their motivations, preferred focus and ambitions alongside your own to develop the best approach for your family. This may mean being more collaborative, but it could also mean taking the lead. If your philanthropic project is meant to unify the family, it is important to take them on the journey with you from the beginning, as you might otherwise achieve the opposite effect. You can explore this topic further in the Family Involvement chapter of the Relationships section of this book.

An engaged family is one where each member's purpose is heard and incorporated in some way. Engaging in the "purpose" conversation with family members may be prudent if, for example:

→ you intend to involve your family in giving;
→ there has been a change in family governance;
→ there has been a liquidity event and your family wants to consider its options.

In order to initiate, change or refine the direction for your philanthropic activities, it might be helpful to start with those family members that will be most closely involved in your philanthropic activity.

Philanthropists give for diverse reasons and with different aims. It is likely that some of these reasons may vary as an individual and, especially, as a family. Reading the compass slightly wrong at the start of your journey can throw you many miles off course in the years ahead or may lead to less favorable outcomes.

The first stage of the navigator will help you to set off in the right direction. Anyone with the desire and resources can give, but our aim is to help you give in a mindful way, with awareness, structure and specific goals: to give with purpose.

For those new to philanthropy, this will help shape the maiden voyage ahead.

For those already active, this reflection offers an opportunity to take stock and re-evaluate your approach, for example, because you might want to:

→ change your course of action;
→ reconsider your activities as you transition from one generation to the next;
→ professionalize your activities and take your giving to the next level;
→ assess and adapt to a change in leadership (either within the family or outside).

To guide you through this important moment of self-reflection, we have separated **PURPOSE** into three components: **Motivation**, **Focus** and **Ambition**.

Introduction 27

Purpose

Motivation

The first step in the *Family Philanthropy Navigator* encourages you to explore and define the motivations behind your giving. There is no "correct" reason to give. In fact, we often observe that families have lots of different motivations. In this context, it's important to know what these are and how to balance them. Why do you and your family want to give? Are you driven by conviction or events? For more experienced philanthropists, has something changed within your family or outside? Is it time to re-evaluate or put your existing reasons to the test? This step will encourage you to define and understand the "why" behind your giving.

Focus

We then shift to examine the focus of your giving. This means moving from understanding the impulses that drive and influence your giving to translating those motivations into the real world. What do you want to do, individually or as a family? What is the scope of your giving? Where is the common ground? For new philanthropists, what causes are you interested in? Who do you want to support? Where do you want to put your resources? This step will help you zoom in on the destination and scope of your philanthropy. For experienced philanthropists, has your focus changed or have the circumstances changed? Do you want to expand your scope of giving?

Ambition

We complete your navigation through the purpose of giving by taking time to consider your ambitions as a philanthropist.
What are you trying to achieve? Do you have specific and measurable targets, such as increasing access to clean water for a certain number of people each year?
Or are your ambitions less tangible and more personal, such as helping to engage the family and to learn and grow together? For already active philanthropists, have your ambitions or expectations changed? This step will allow you to outline your goals and expectations, but also to start thinking about how to manage your structures and relationships before you start to give.

Insight

BE FLEXIBLE

Things change, and as you venture into your philanthropic activities you will also test your assumptions and hypothesis. While it is vital to define your focus and ambitions in a clear and concise manner, it is important to build flexibility into your thinking and your approach. You may need to refine or adjust your focus if circumstances change (or because you want to respond to an immediate crisis). You may need to go back to the drawing board if you find that your ambitions are not realistic or achievable.

Introduction

Purpose

Motivation

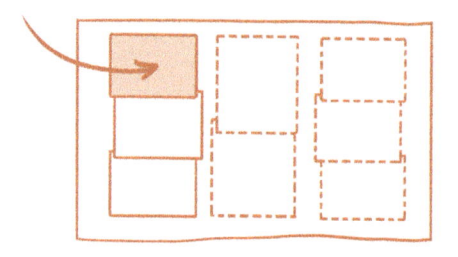

Setting the Scene

There are many reasons why people give and the reasons for becoming a philanthropist are mostly very personal.

You might want your name to be remembered or recognized for doing something good or for having helped alleviate some pain in the world. You might give because of your faith and religious beliefs. It could also be that you have overcome a challenge or crisis and want to help others overcome, or prevent them from experiencing, the same challenge – using philanthropy to right a wrong in the world. You might want to give in order to have maximum impact related to a specific problem.

Different motivations are not mutually exclusive. You and your family may regard multiple motivations as relevant and important. Irrespective of what your motivations are, it is crucial that you and your family are aware of the full spectrum of points of view, so that you can plan accordingly. Once you activate your giving, the time, money and other resources you dedicate cannot be retrieved. In this light, ideally, your motivations should be well thought through, clear and understood by all involved.

As the architect of your family's philanthropic journey and the guardian of your family's legacy, you carry the responsibility for setting the right course, achieving results and taking people with you. Spelling out your motivations and communicating them effectively will help you get off on the right foot.

This step in the navigator will help you and your family define the "why" behind your giving. There are no perfect answers and there are always tensions and trade-offs. You will also need to consider the wider picture of your family and partners. A collaborative approach will inspire more engagement and enable you to better define your ambitions and the structure of your giving.

Setting the Compass

Before coming to any conclusions, you may want to reflect on a number of trade-offs, conundrums and dilemmas to define the real motivation behind your giving. These tensions will help you to explore the complex reasons for your desire to give, and the factors at play. They will also help you surface different views and perceptions that individual family members might have. Your answers are likely to be complex and there might also by hybrid solutions – hence the need to explore them now and in depth.

Purpose

INTRINSIC ――┼―┼―┼――┼―┼―┼―― **EXTRINSIC**

Personal factors such as values and beliefs, passion and the joy of giving

Identify all the factors that might influence your motivation for giving. It is likely that there will be mix of intrinsic (personal) and extrinsic (business, peer, family) forces at play, although some may not be as important as others. Understanding these elements and their relative importance will help you to align family and partners, and to design the right goals and approach for your giving.

Pragmatic, external forces such as reputation, image, and peer pressure

→ Are you **passionate** about a **specific subject** or **cause**?
→ What **beliefs** and **values** drive you?
→ Are you **motivated** by the simple joy of **giving**?
→ Are you driven by a desire to **give back to society**?
→ Is **image** and **reputation** important to you?
→ Are there any financial and tax **considerations**?

NOTES

_____
_____
_____
_____

Family Philanthropy Navigator

ALTRUISM ├──┼──┼──┼──┼──┼──┼──┼──┤ **SELF-INTEREST**

Self-less care for others and philanthropic causes even if there is a cost

It is common for family philanthropy to be inspired by a blend of altruistic and "selfish" reasons. In our experience, most families who give are driven predominantly by altruism, and, therefore, lean to the left of this spectrum. However, effective giving also requires a pragmatic approach to relationships and resource management. While philanthropy, by definition, is naturally altruistic, more and more families also want to see some form of "return on investment" to ensure that they are making a difference.

Giving purely to derive specific personal, family, and/or business benefits

→ Are you giving purely out of **compassion or empathy** (altruism)?
→ Are you fully focused on the **impact on the ground**?
→ Do you want to take on a less **visible role**, or do you enjoy being in the limelight?
→ Do you hope to achieve some form of **personal benefit** from giving?
→ Are you giving as a way to **promote** your family or business brand and values?

NOTES

Purpose

LEGACY DRIVEN ├─┼─┼─┼─┼─┼─┼─┼─┼─┤ **NOVEL**

Preserving and transferring family traditions, values and/or existing philanthropic activities

Your family may or may not have an existing philanthropic footprint or journey. Nonetheless, many families see giving as a way to protect and share their legacy, traditions or values, especially when it comes to involving the next generation. There may be a desire to adapt to new and changing circumstances by taking a fresh approach to family giving. After all, solutions that worked well in the past may not work quite as well in today's rapidly changing world.

Changing direction and/or starting a new journey through novel or different philanthropic activities

→ Is your impulse to give **inspired** by family traditions and established practices?
→ Are you **experienced** in giving, or a senior family member and want to pass on values to the next generation?
→ Do you want to onboard the **next generation**?
→ Have circumstances and **expectations** changed?
→ Are you a next generation family member taking over responsibility or wanting to make your mark?
→ Are you **looking** at **exploring** or supporting new philanthropic activities where your family wasn't active before?

NOTES

Insight

FROM GIVING TO GIVING BACK

Our reasons for giving can change throughout our lives. Younger individuals may be driven more by a sense of responsibility to use their privileges and skills to change the world. A philanthropist in middle age may start to think they should give something back to society. An older philanthropist may be more concerned with the legacy they leave behind. The stage of life you are in can shape your giving and warrants reflection as part of your journey towards defining your motivations.

Motivation   35

Purpose

Insight

EVENTS AND FINANCES

The status of our finances and life events can often trigger the impulse to give. An entrepreneur may have accumulated a certain level of wealth through the growth of a business or after having sold the business; there might have been an extraordinary shareholder dividend payment; there may have been a change in family governance; or a recent inheritance event. Irrespective of the source of the financial resource, consider aligning your financial situation with your purpose before starting your philanthropic journey.

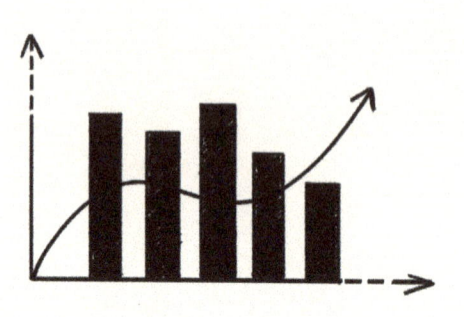

WHAT COMES FIRST: CAUSE, FAMILY OR BUSINESS?

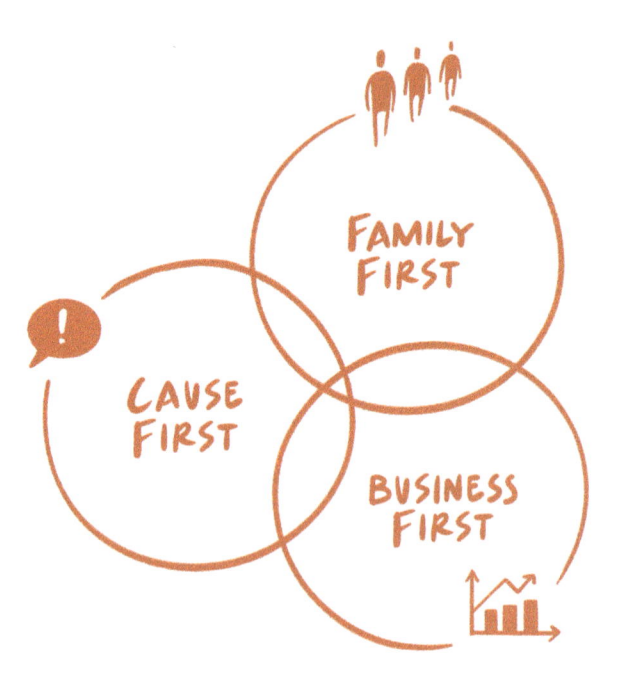

It is useful to reflect on where the main emphasis of the motivation for giving lies between the causes you want to address, your family and business – as well as how those different influences interact. While it could be that you and your family are only driven by one of these three sources of motivation, it is likely that the true motivation is a combination of these different factors, with an emphasis on helping others. However, there is typically one dominant factor that drives individuals or families to engage in philanthropy.

Family Philanthropy Navigator

CAUSE FIRST

- How important are **causes** in your motivation to give?
- To what extent do you want to support a **specific cause** or address a **specific problem** or **challenge**?
- What **specific** cause(s) are you deeply **passionate** about?

FAMILY FIRST

- How significant are **family factors** in your motivations for giving?
- To what extent do you want to **unite** the family, to **onboard** the next generation or to **include** family members who are not working in the business but should be **active contributors** to the family enterprise system?
- Do you want to **leverage** philanthropy to **transfer** and **manage** your wealth?
- Do you want to **leave a legacy**?

BUSINESS FIRST

- Are **business** factors the **dominant** drivers of your giving?
- To what extent, as a business owner, do you want to **leverage synergies** with your business or to offer employees an **opportunity** to get involved in philanthropic projects?
- Do you want to win the **respect** and **goodwill** of specific **institutions** or **partners**?
- Do you want to **boost** the **brand** and **reputation** of your business or **benefit** from monetary **incentive** schemes?

NOTES

Purpose

Activities

Now that you have explored the wider considerations for the motivation step in the navigator, it is time to define the "why" of philanthropy.

In this section, we provide you with simple, yet important, activities that will help you make decisions around this very personal aspect of giving, and to answer the key navigator questions that conclude this chapter.

While there are many reasons why people engage in philanthropy, studies have revealed patterns and similarities that we can use to categorize these motivations. Doing so can help us understand and pinpoint our own motivations as well as those of our family members.

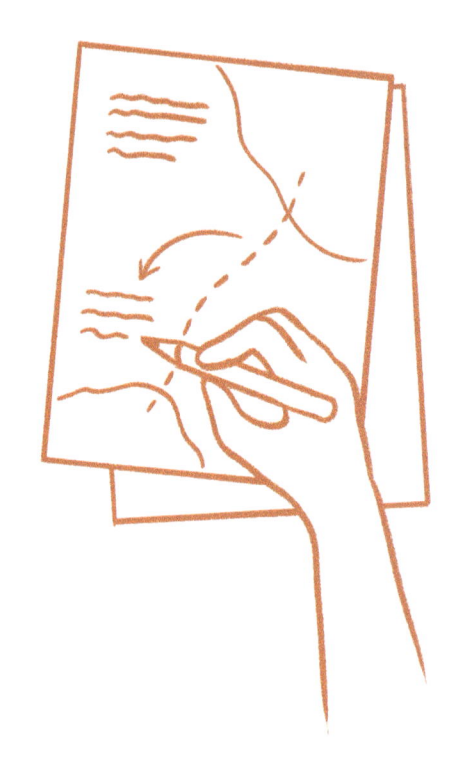

Family Philanthropy Navigator **Questions:**

→ What is our motivation?
→ What inspires us to give?
→ What drives us to give now or continue giving?

Activity 1:
Review the Trade-Offs

Step 1

Review the trade-offs presented earlier in this chapter and, individually, answer the following questions. Use different colors to highlight your response to the two questions as they relate to each of the trade-offs. You can position yourself anywhere along the spectrum, from one end to the other.

1. **Where is our philanthropy today?**
2. **Where would I like our philanthropy to be in the future?**

Step 2

As a family, compare and discuss where each one of you marked dots for "where are we today" and "where would we like to be." What are the similarities and differences? Where are you aligned or not? How can this further shape your journey?

Step 3

If there are any differences in your perspectives, discuss how you wish to address these.

* Note to aspiring philanthropists:
If you are not yet philanthropically active you can simply focus on question 2 in Step 1.

Motivation

Purpose

Activity 2:
Defining Your Reasons for Giving

Step 1

Each family member should identify their top three reasons for giving. The list of statements on page 41 might help you in identifying your reasons for giving.

Step 2

Assign your top motivations to the different circles in the following diagram. Your motivations can be positioned anywhere in the diagram, including at the intersections of different circles.

Step 3

The results should be shared and discussed as a family and then refined to create your core family motivations for giving. This will help you and your family make sense of the "why" behind your philanthropy and ultimately help you organize your giving effectively.

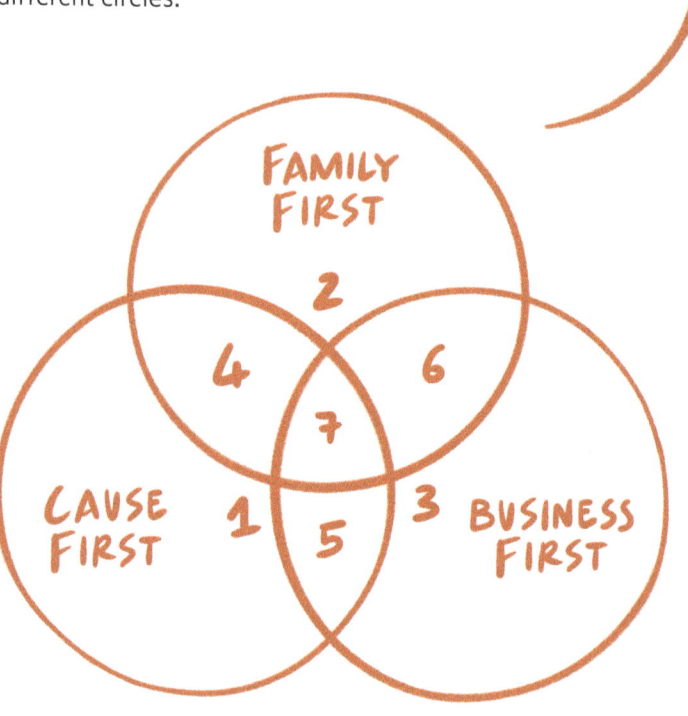

Venn diagram with three overlapping circles labeled FAMILY FIRST, CAUSE FIRST, and BUSINESS FIRST. Regions numbered: 1 (Cause First only), 2 (Family First only), 3 (Business First only), 4 (Cause First ∩ Family First), 5 (Cause First ∩ Business First), 6 (Family First ∩ Business First), 7 (all three).

40   Family Philanthropy Navigator

LIST OF STATEMENTS

This non-exhaustive list of statements will offer some guidance in your reflection for Activity 2.

- → I am aware of specific, underserved needs and wish to address them with my giving.
- → I genuinely care about others and act out of compassion and empathy.
- → My main motivation is driven by my values and beliefs.
- → My desire to give was driven by an external event (e.g. a natural disaster, a pandemic, a war).
- → I want to give something back to society.
- → I had a profound personal experience that has opened my eyes.
- → I enjoy giving and find pleasure in helping others.
- → I wish to make a difference and change the world for the better.
- → I wish to leave behind a personal or family legacy.
- → Philanthropy is a way to reconcile family members and involve the broader family.
- → I want to leverage philanthropy as a tool to involve the next generation or transfer values to the next generation.
- → My giving is primarily driven by incoming requests for support.
- → I wish to strengthen my personal, my family's and/or our business' reputation and image.
- → I see philanthropy as a tool to recruit and retain top talent in the organization.
- → Philanthropy offers our employees an opportunity to contribute to the greater good.
- → I want to leverage synergies between our business and philanthropy.

Purpose

Focus

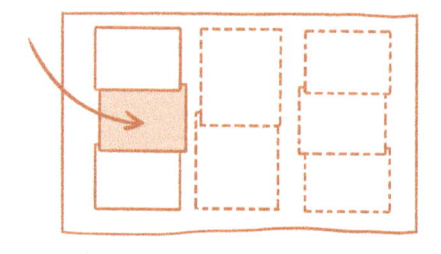

Setting the Scene

Having explored the motivations behind your desire to give, it is time to decide what kind of causes you and your family would like to support – the focus of your giving.

In today's uncertain world, there is an almost infinite number of needs for philanthropists to address. Depending on what drives you to be philanthropically active, you might already have identified a specific problem or cause. For example, if someone in your family has suffered from a disease and your motivation is to help others who suffer from, or to prevent, that disease, your focus is pretty clear. In other cases, you might approach philanthropy more broadly and work through a list of different possibilities before deciding which causes to focus on.

The "Focus" stage in the navigator provides a platform to make choices about the causes, scope and final port of call for your giving. For the novice, this a voyage of discovery; for the established philanthropist, it's an opportunity to conduct a check on the current focus of activities and, if necessary, consider a change of direction.

In order to frame the choices available to you, we recommend referring to the UN SDGs, which were adopted by all UN Member States in 2015 as "a universal call to action to end poverty, protect the planet and ensure that all people enjoy peace and prosperity by 2030."

These 17 goals cover a range of focus areas from poverty and climate change to peace building and equal rights. Increasingly, we observe that embracing the common language and widely recognized framework of the UN SDGs enables diverse actors from across the giving spectrum to align

42 **Family Philanthropy Navigator**

their activities, build partnerships and maximize their impact.

Making a decision about where to focus takes time, research and careful consideration. It could require the involvement and agreement of family members, who may have different views and interests. It may help to discuss these early on and seek solutions that will promote engagement. Perhaps it may require adopting different avenues to achieve different aims amongst the family, or perhaps you can align your interests and efforts behind one core focus for giving.

Insight

DO YOUR RESEARCH

It is crucial to do some due diligence and research when answering the question "what" or "to/for whom" in giving. This can be a personal undertaking, a joint effort with family or outsourced to an adviser. Does the destination for your giving require the kind of support you think it does? Giving is a partnership, if done well, with benefits for all parties. Like all partnerships, it is best to work together with a shared purpose from the start. By understanding the specific needs of your chosen focus areas, you will lay the foundations for more effective and rewarding giving.

Purpose

Setting the Compass

By reflecting on the following trade-offs and dilemmas, you will be able to explore and define the focus of your giving. The more specific you can be in this section, the better. If you are interested in environmental causes, for example, does that mean you want to work with a small NGO to help protect black rhinos in Namibia, offer to plant more trees in your community, or to partner with a large advocacy organization to fund a global awareness campaign about climate change?

Insight

GETTING YOUR FOCUS RIGHT

Giving is choosing. It is worth thinking about how to align your motivation for giving with the interests and topics you and your family are passionate about, not just the needs that you see or hear about in the world. If you can align both your motivation, interests and the causes you want to support, it can help to sustain engagement and deliver better outcomes.

DEPTH ———|—|—|—|—|—|—|— **BREADTH**

Supporting a specific cause or project in one area

Considering the relationship between the depth and breadth of your giving helps to ensure your aims, partners, resources and structures are aligned. If you are driven towards depth of impact, you might focus all of your giving on a specific cause, such as helping unemployed women in their local community transfer to the labor market. If it's all about breadth, you might want to share efforts across a number of organizations working in diverse fields. This could be influenced by differing or common interests within the family.

Spreading your support across diverse causes and projects across a multitude of areas

→ What are your **interests** and **passions** as a family?
→ Do you want to **support** only one specific cause as a family?
→ Are you more interested in spreading your giving across a range of **different causes** and activities, such as education, healthcare, arts?
→ Are there **differing interests** between family members that might require a **blended approach**?

NOTES

_____
_____
_____
_____

44 Family Philanthropy Navigator

ROOT CAUSE /SYSTEM CHANGE ⊢────┼───┼───┼───┼───┼───┼───┼─── **EFFECT /SYMPTOMS**

Directly addressing the root cause or trigger point of an issue or problem

There are many ways to tackle the focus areas of your giving – from seeking to address the root causes to reducing the symptoms of an issue. Sometimes it makes sense to focus on the symptoms, for example, backing an emergency appeal during a pandemic to provide critical support when it is most needed. On the other hand, many philanthropists are keen to focus their giving on solutions that lead to lasting change. Take a family who wants to make a difference for dementia patients, perhaps inspired by personal experience. They could tackle the root causes and fund medical research, they could support initiatives that make life easier for dementia patients and their families or they could blend both approaches.

Focusing on ways to treat or reduce the symptoms of an issue or problem

→ Do you want to **focus** on the cause or **effect** of a certain issue?
→ Are there **compelling reasons** for addressing the symptoms?
→ Does it make more sense to tackle the **root causes**?
→ Could you take a **twin approach**?

NOTES
_____
_____
_____
_____

Focus

Purpose

LOCAL ├┼┼┼┼─┼┼┼┼┤ **GLOBAL**

Giving to causes and projects on a local level only

You might have a specific connection to a certain community, due to personal, family or business reasons, and want to align your giving accordingly, such as supporting schools close to your business operations. You may be more interested in giving on a wider scale to, for example, alleviate poverty or tackle climate change. In practice, families might give across a range of geographies for different reasons. The regionality of your giving could also include multiple levels, such as your community, your city, your state, your country, your continent and globally. It could also be a combination of different local areas such as providing access to clean sanitation in villages in India.

Supporting more general and globally relevant causes

→ Is your giving **focused on a specific geographic region**?
→ Are you focusing on **global issues**?
→ Are there **several areas** that are of **particular interest** to you?

Insight

REMEMBER YOUR MOTIVATION

The focus of any giving can be triggered by your motivation. If you are inspired to give because you have lost a relative to a terminal illness, then it follows that the treatment for or research into that disease could be the focus of your giving, as well as bringing family members together. Try to keep sight of your motivation as you refine your focus.

SOLUTION PUSH ⊢―⊢―⊢―⊢―⊢―⊢―⊢―⊢ **NEED PULL**

Seeking to solve or address a problem or issue by creating and delivering your own solution

Today, we observe that giving is trending more towards a "need pull" approach rather than "solution push" as more philanthropists seek to work closely with partners to harness their expertise and more effectively address the needs of their beneficiaries. A cautionary tale about the limitations of the "solution push" approach can be seen in the distribution of mosquito nets to rural communities which were intended to tackle malaria but were, in some circumstances, deployed as fishing nets with damaging effects on small fish populations.

Seeking a solution by engaging closely with beneficiaries or partners to understand their needs deeply

→ Are you trying to make a difference by applying a **pre-ordained solution** to a situation of your choosing?
→ Are you giving primarily based on your **personal beliefs**, **preferences** and **expertise**?
→ Are you driven to give by **external requests** and **solicitations**?
→ Are you engaging with individuals and organizations on the ground to **understand** their specific **needs**?

✏️ NOTES

_____
_____
_____
_____

Focus

Purpose

BUSINESS RELATED ——|——|——|——|——|——|——|——|—— **BUSINESS UNRELATED**

Aligning your giving purely with your core business activities

It can make sense to channel your giving in a way that aligns with your business activities, perhaps to harness professional expertise and networks or to foster a more cohesive approach across your family enterprise system. For example, you might be a family owning a healthcare company that wants to support hospitals or a high net worth banker who wants to offer microfinance to low-income entrepreneurs in emerging economies. However, you might want to look beyond the specific business ecosystem to enable your family members to explore different areas of interest.

Giving to causes and projects that have no link to your business

- → Is your giving **related to your business** activities?
- → Are there any **potential synergies** between your business and your philanthropic activities?
- → Do you want to **engage company team** members in your giving?
- → Do you prefer to focus your giving on areas that sit **outside of your business** focus or industry?

NOTES

_____
_____
_____
_____

48 Family Philanthropy Navigator

Insight

LEARNING FROM THE PAST

History shows that the traditional top-down method of charitable giving has often struggled to yield sustainable results. Often, it can be counter-productive and disruptive to take expertise or solutions from one part of the world and assume that they will translate into benefits elsewhere. We recommend researching and working with your giving partners in a more holistic way.

Purpose

Activities

Once you have completed your reflection on the causes, scope and destination of your giving, it is time to make some initial commitments if this is your first journey in giving, or to consider a change of course if you are already engaged in philanthropy. The following exercises will provide structure and guidance to help you complete the concluding navigator questions and continue your evolving journey in philanthropy.

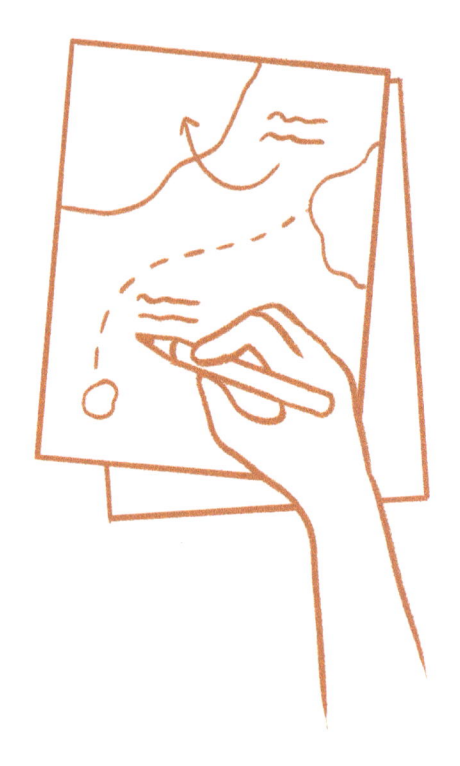

> *Family Philanthropy Navigator*
> **Questions:**
>
> → What is our focus?
> → What causes are we passionate about?
> → In which regions do we give/want to give?
> → Who or what ultimately benefits from our giving?

Activity 1:
Review the Trade-Offs

Step 1

Review the various trade-offs in this chapter and, individually, answer the following questions. Use different colors to highlight where you stand in relation to the two questions in each of the trade-offs. You can position yourself anywhere along the spectrum, from one end to the other end of the trade-off.

1. **Where is our philanthropy today?**
2. **Where would I like our philanthropy to be in the future?**

Step 2

As a family, compare and discuss where each one of you positioned the dots for "where are we today" and "where would we like to be". What are the similarities and differences? Where are you aligned or not? How can this further shape your journey?

Step 3

If there are any differences in your perspectives, discuss how you wish to address these.

* Note to aspiring philanthropists:
If you are not yet philanthropically active you can simply focus on question 2 in Step 1.

Purpose

Activity 2:
Choosing Your Cause

Step 1

Go through the list of the 17 UN SDGs below and select the top three areas that you are passionate about. You can refer to the UN website for further information about each goal. In addition, we also provide a list of philanthropic causes for you to consider as a source of inspiration. This is not an exhaustive list so feel free to suggest other options as you see fit.

1. No Poverty
2. Zero Hunger
3. Good Health and Well-Being
4. Quality Education
5. Gender Equality
6. Clean Water and Sanitation
7. Affordable and Clean Energy
8. Decent Work and Economic Growth
9. Industry, Innovation and Infrastructure
10. Reduced Inequalities
11. Sustainable Cities and Communities
12. Responsible Consumption and Production
13. Climate Action
14. Life Below Water
15. Life on Land
16. Peace, Justice and Strong Institutions
17. Partnerships for the Goals

52   **Family Philanthropy Navigator**

CAUSES TO CONSIDER

HUMAN RELIEF

- → Child protection
- → Demographic change (rural exodus, etc.)
- → Disaster relief
- → Migration and refugee crises
- → Post-conflict support

SOCIETAL CAUSES

- → Arts
- → Culture
- → Music
- → Medical research
- → Religion
- → Science
- → Sport

SOCIAL AND ECONOMIC DEVELOPMENT

- → Civil rights
- → Community development
- → Domestic violence
- → Disability
- → Education
- → Food and drinkable water
- → Gender equality
- → Healthcare
- → Human rights
- → Income generation
- → Mental health
- → Poverty alleviation
- → Sustainable economic growth
- → Youth causes (vocational training, employment, etc.)

ENVIRONMENT

- → Agriculture and fishing
- → Air pollution
- → Clean energy
- → Endangered species conservation
- → Forestry
- → Global warming
- → Nature conservation
- → Protection of biodiversity
- → Scarcity of natural resources
- → Water pollution

ADVOCACY

- → Change in political arena
- → Conflict and peace
- → International diplomacy
- → Political instability
- → Populism

Purpose

Step 2

Once you have chosen your potential causes, think about which geographic regions you wish to be active in: globally, regionally, specific countries or communities.

Step 3

Think about exactly whom or what you wish to help with your giving. Factors to consider include age, gender, populations, races, ethnic groups, or also animals, natural habitats, etc. Shortlist your top three causes in the table below.

Step 4

Describe why you feel that these causes are important and that you and your family should address them. Why are you passionate about them? Continue working with the table below.

SHORTLIST CAUSES	WHY DID YOU SELECT THIS CAUSE? WHY ARE YOU PASSIONATE ABOUT THIS CAUSE?
1.	
2.	
3.	

Step 5

As a family, discuss all your selected causes and try to create a shortlist of your family's top three causes.

Step 6

Formulate your philanthropic mission statement. The more specific your focus of giving is, the easier it gets to formulate this statement. A mission statement is important when you are speaking with others about your philanthropic activities. A good statement should be short, simple, specific, ambitious and easy to remember or to associate with you.

Here are some examples of mission statements from the case studies featured at the end of the Purpose section:

FOUNDATION	MISSION STATEMENT
Eva Ahlström Foundation	Our mission is to support organizations, societies or individual persons in Finland and abroad, with a good and documented reputation, to work globally and locally to support women, children and others that are in an exposed situation due to poverty, oppression, war, political instability, natural disasters or other difficult circumstances.
Tsao Ng Yu Shun Foundation	Our mission is to advance a positive transformation of the aging experience, we seek mindset and systemic change by implementing innovation in community-based eldercare, training and education, policy relevant research, collaboration and advocacy.
Fondation Juniclair	The mission of the Juniclair Foundation is to support and assist development projects in the areas of education, the environment, women's rights and violence prevention.

Focus

Purpose

Ambition

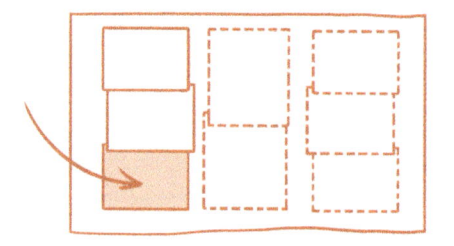

Setting the Scene

The final stage in the Purpose section of the navigator explores the ambitions behind your giving. What do you want to achieve? This stage is about taking the implicit and making it explicit – defining your aims and expectations.

There are different ways to view success and some ambitions are broader or harder to define than others. There is also a difference between the quantifiable hard outcomes of giving and more qualitative longer term impacts. Irrespective of what your motivations and focus are, it is advisable to reflect on and try to spell out what success means for you and your family, knowing that it is a lot easier to do this for some causes than for others.

It is also well worth reflecting on the wider implications of your giving and the broader impact your actions can have before you begin to give. For example, you could want to complete a single project, such as restoring an old theater, or generate something more sustainable that has knock-on effects. If you want to improve access to quality education for children in rural Mexico, do you want to meet specific grade targets for a fixed number of students, set attendance goals or aim for a certain number of university places or good quality employment in the future?

Not all philanthropists want to define explicit KPIs as a means to measure the results of their giving. This can be because they want their giving to take a similar path to more traditional charitable giving. However, we argue that it still makes sense to define in some way your level of ambition.

Ambition is not just about the final destination of your resources. It is also about what you want to achieve as an individual or, collectively, as a family. Do you want to improve family relations and decision making or preserve values across generations? Do you want to empower the next generation?

Ambition ties in closely with your and your family's motivation and focus. When you know why you want to give and where you want to focus, your ambitions should fall into place collectively alongside the other two elements of purpose.

We also recommend that you approach this chapter with half an eye on the Impact chapter that concludes the *Family Philanthropy Navigator*. Impact and ambition have an inevitably close relationship and should be considered as two parts of the same whole.

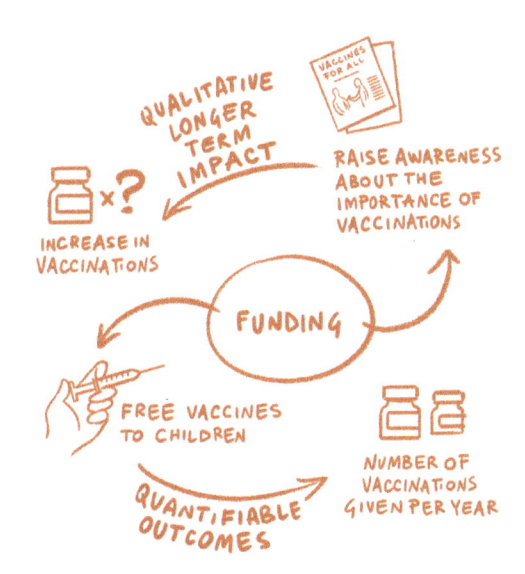

EXAMPLES

→ Funding a project that offers free vaccines to children in a certain part of the world, where you can count the number of vaccinations given per year (**quantifiable outcomes**).

→ Funding a project to raise awareness of the importance of vaccinations, where you will need to look at more long-term changes in human behavior without knowing whether an increase in vaccinations was the direct result of your giving (**qualitative longer-term impact**).

Ambition

Purpose

Setting the Compass

By exploring the range of ways to measure ambition and success, you and your family can either set expectations for new giving or reassess and realign goals for your existing and future philanthropic activities.

NOTES

DRIVEN BY STORYTELLING, NARRATIVE ———————————— **DRIVEN BY MEASUREMENTS AND TARGETS**

Seeking and sharing stories, experiences and cases to illustrate and understand needs and causes

In a data-driven world, more and more philanthropists use data and statistics to set KPIs or targets, ensure the effective use of resources and to work towards their ambitions. But storytelling and sharing experiences can prove just as valuable, especially when seeking support from family members or giving partners something to celebrate. You may want to specify, for example, the target number of polio vaccines to be delivered per year or the target number of trees to be planted in the Amazon. At the same time, it may be just as important to document case studies about the improved quality of life for children vaccinated against polio or the inspiring story from a day living in an indigenous Amazonian village to showcase the importance of planting and protecting trees in that part of the world.

Establishing KPIs and adopting data-driven approaches to design interventions

→ What do you aim to achieve with our philanthropic activities?
→ What does success in philanthropy mean to you and your family?
→ How small or big, generic or focused, do you want to be with your giving?
→ Are you more interested in creating case studies and sharing stories, or is adopting a data-driven approach your preferred choice?
→ How important is quantitative and qualitative information in the realization of your ambitions?

STRATEGIC /COHESIVE ├─┼─┼─┼─┼─┼─┼─┼─┼─┤ **AD HOC /REACTIVE**

Planning fully funded and long-term oriented strategic giving that is aligned with the vision, mission and activities of the family enterprise system

It is possible to structure your giving in a highly organized and cohesive way that harmonizes with your family enterprise system. You might prefer to be extremely agile and independent, free to give on the spur of the moment if the need arises. For families with a developed enterprise system, it can make sense to integrate any philanthropic giving into that ecosystem. However, it can also be worthwhile to create leeway for a more reactive approach, so that family members can respond to requests and emergency situations.

Spontaneously responding to incoming requests or specific causes that require support

→ Is your giving in line with an **overarching strategy** for giving, either personally, as a family, or as a business?
→ Do you want your giving to be **cohesive** and **consistent** across the board?
→ Do you want to **proactively go** out and **seek** projects and causes to support, which are aligned with your strategy and vision?
→ Do you want to be able to **respond spontaneously** in incoming requests or a crisis in the world?

NOTES

_____
_____
_____
_____

Ambition

Purpose

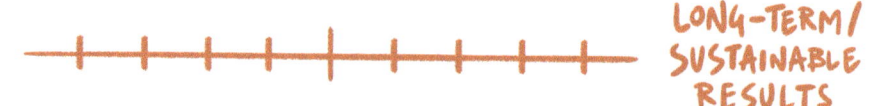

IMMEDIATE RESULTS ├─┼─┼─┼─┼─┼─┼─┤ **LONG-TERM/ SUSTAINABLE RESULTS**

Provide support designed to mitigate short-term problems

Impact can be measured in the short and long term. In today's world, most philanthropists want to achieve a lasting impact through their giving to try to eliminate the causes of, rather than temporarily address the symptoms of, social, economic and environmental problems. It is also important to feel like you are getting long-term value in return for your resources. However, there may be occasions when immediate action can be just as impactful, for example, providing funding to food banks in an economic downturn, supporting victims from a tsunami or earthquake, or offering free vaccines to vulnerable communities during a pandemic.

Provide support designed to deliver long-term, lasting change

→ Do you and your family prefer to work on **systemic matters** to achieve lasting impact or support causes that need **immediate response**?
→ Is your giving **focused** on **immediate results** in order to alleviate a specific pain?
→ Are you trying to have a more **long-term** and **sustainable** impact?

NOTES

_____
_____
_____
_____

60 Family Philanthropy Navigator

Insight

CAN IT BE MEASURED?

We recommend embracing complexity and aiming for a balance between qualitative and quantitative ways to assess the end result of your giving. If you want to measure your impact, then business-style KPIs with fixed timeframes can help to provide clarity and structure. However, less tangible ambitions – such as transferring family values, sharing knowledge with other relevant players by taking a role on the board of various organizations, or raising awareness about a burning issue – may be best judged in a less fixed way over a longer period of time.

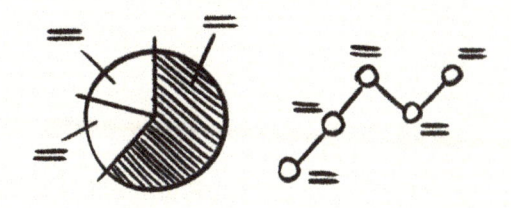

Insight

CONSIDER MULTIPLE FACTORS

When it comes to giving, it is important to reflect on the balance of ambitions and expectations that exist between you, your family, your business and society. How will you balance your personal ambitions against those of your siblings or children? Will your business interests affect the way you give and what you want to achieve? Are there societal factors that should influence your actions and goals as a family or business?

Ambition   61

Purpose

SOCIO-ECONOMIC OR ENVIRONMENTAL RETURNS ONLY

┼─┼─┼─┼─┼─┼─┼─┼─┼

INCLUDING FINANCIAL RETURNS

Giving in a traditional way with no expectation of a financial return, focusing only on socio-economic or environmental benefits

Your ambitions for giving determine the kind of "return on investment" you are looking for. For many philanthropists, this often means expecting no other return than positive effect on the ground through their donation and mobilization of other resources. A more innovative approach to giving has introduced an investor-driven mindset that can have some appeal to many enterprising families, depending on their purpose and circumstances.

Embracing alternative forms of giving that blend socio-economic and/or environmental with financial returns, such as venture philanthropy and impact investment

→ Is your giving **embedded** in **traditional philanthropy** to support, for example, social or environmental causes?
→ Are you considering **social investments** or **venture philanthropy** as options for your giving?
→ Do you want to support social enterprises that have a positive impact, while also offering a **potential** financial return?
→ Will you apply **innovative ways** of giving to achieve greater impact, effectiveness and efficiency?

Insight

QUANTIFY YOUR AMBITION

As you define your ambition, think about the different ways you can have an impact with the resources at your disposal. By contemplating the extent of your ambition, you can manage expectations and resources effectively. Do you support 10,000 young mothers in India for one year or would there be more meaningful impact from helping 1,000 mothers for ten years?

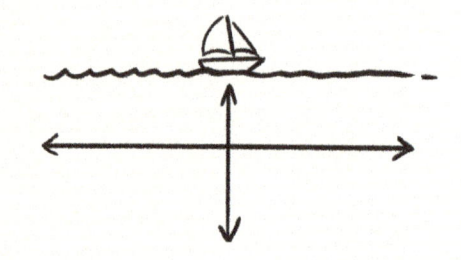

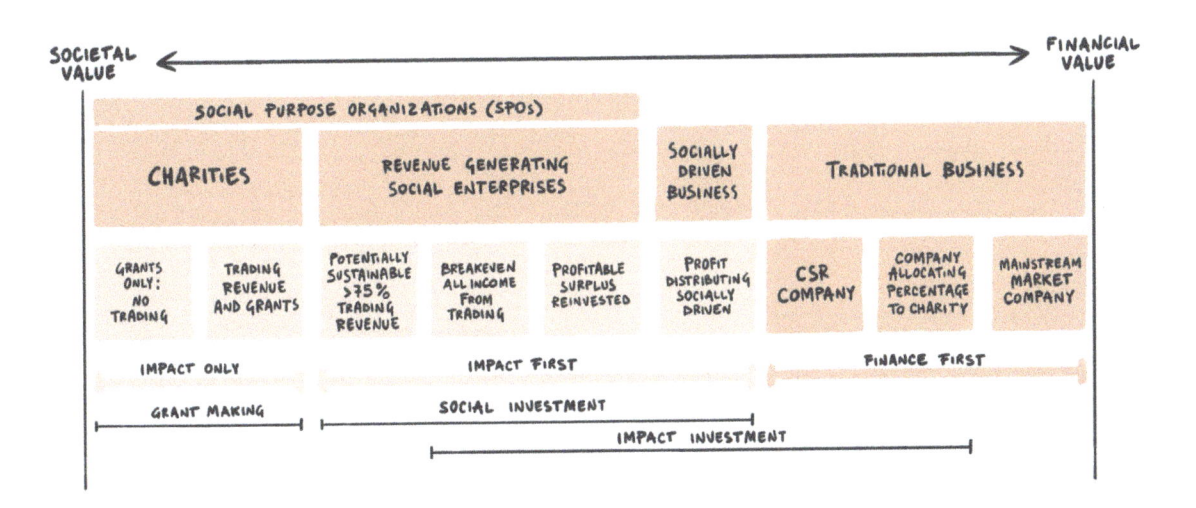

The Investment Spectrum

SOCIETAL VALUE ←——————————————————————————————→ **FINANCIAL VALUE**

SOCIAL PURPOSE ORGANIZATIONS (SPOS)

CHARITIES	REVENUE GENERATING SOCIAL ENTERPRISES	SOCIALLY DRIVEN BUSINESS	TRADITIONAL BUSINESS
GRANTS ONLY: NO TRADING / TRADING REVENUE AND GRANTS	POTENTIALLY SUSTAINABLE >75% TRADING REVENUE / BREAKEVEN ALL INCOME FROM TRADING / PROFITABLE SURPLUS REINVESTED	PROFIT DISTRIBUTING SOCIALLY DRIVEN	CSR COMPANY / COMPANY ALLOCATING PERCENTAGE TO CHARITY / MAINSTREAM MARKET COMPANY

IMPACT ONLY — IMPACT FIRST — FINANCE FIRST

GRANT MAKING — SOCIAL INVESTMENT — IMPACT INVESTMENT

As you are reflecting on the right model for your giving, you might want to consider the investment spectrum, which ranges from purely charitable giving all the way to traditional business and investing. While the righthand end of the spectrum is not directly linked to the core concept of philanthropy, it still makes sense to consider where your various activities are positioned along this spectrum to establish the best approach, in line with your and your family's overarching vision, mission and values.

You may not need or want to spread your activities across the entire spectrum. Some families engage in a variety of ways at points across the spectrum while others position themselves only at the ends of the spectrum – making money through the business and giving through traditional charity.

Ambition 63

Purpose

Activities

Now that you have reflected on the factors that can guide the ambitions behind your philanthropy, it is time to outline what they are, so that you can move to the next stages of the navigator. The following activities and concluding navigator questions will help you define your ambitions. The outcome will also inform the activity in the Impact chapter, where you will define your impact strategy.

Family Philanthropy Navigator Questions:

→ What are our ambitions?
→ What do we aim to achieve?
→ What does success look like for us?

Activity 1:
Review the Trade-Offs

Step 1

Review the trade-offs in this chapter and, individually, answer the following questions. Use different colors to visually highlight where you stand in relation to the two questions in each of the trade-offs. You can position yourself anywhere along the spectrum from one end to the other end of the trade-off.

1. **Where is our philanthropy today?**
2. **Where would I like our philanthropy to be in the future?**

Step 2

As a family, compare and discuss where each one of you positioned the dots for "where are we today" and "where would we like to be". What are the similarities and differences? Where are you aligned or not? How can this further shape your journey?

Step 3

If there are any differences in your perspectives, discuss how you wish to address these.

* Note to aspiring philanthropists:
If you are not yet philanthropically active you can simply focus on question 2 in Step 1.

Ambition 65

Purpose

**Activity 2:
Define Your Ambition**

Step 1

Write down what success means to you. What needs to happen so that you will feel like your philanthropic activity is worth pursuing?

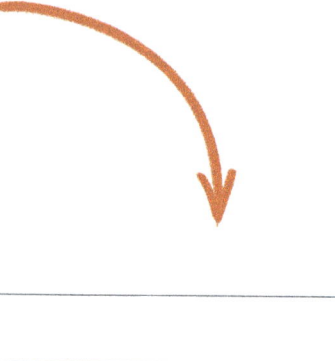

Step 2

Each family member should share what they wrote down in Step 1. Through a discussion, assess to what extent you and your family share an understanding of what success means.

Step 3

As a family, think about how you might be able to measure success. Reflect back on the qualitative versus quantitative metrics of success introduced earlier in this chapter. You can either start with an individual brainstorming exercise and then share and discuss in the group, or you can immediately engage in a group discussion.

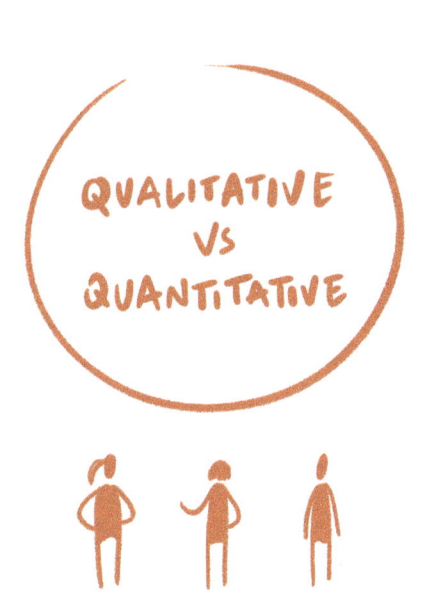

Ambition 67

Purpose

Case Study
The Eva Ahlström Foundation

In Conversation with Maria Ahlström-Bondestam

"Together we created something new from existing family values and history."

→ **Name:** Maria Ahlström-Bondestam, Co-Founder and Chair of the Eva Ahlström Foundation

→ **Country of origin:** Finland

→ **Family size (total number of family members):** 420 family members (including in-laws) over seven generations

→ **Background information about your family's legacy and current business activities:** My great-great-grandfather Antti Ahlström started our family business in 1851 in timber trading, sawmill operations and shipping. Today our portfolio companies operate in 29 countries with 15,500 employees and annual net sales EUR 5 billion. Our roots can still be seen in our biggest public listed portfolio company Ahlstrom-Munksjö which provides innovative and sustainable fiber solutions. We also have operations in industrial technology, real estate and forest.

→ **Which generation are you part of?** 5th generation

→ **Number of family members involved in your philanthropic activities:** 25 women in the 5th generation co-founded the Eva Ahlström Foundation in 2010. The foundation today has several satellites as well as an international chapter based in Geneva. Approx. 20–25 family members are actively involved in our philanthropic activities that is supported by the whole family.

Family Philanthropy Navigator

Areas of giving

Focus of Giving
We support underprivileged women, children and families.

Country/Region
We are active in Finland and internationally, preferably in communities where we have businesses or history.

Other Aspects Worth Noting
Collectively, we have three active foundations. Recently, we merged another family branch's foundation into the Eva Ahlström Foundation to accumulate resources and to have a greater impact. We appointed one relative from that branch to the board of the Eva Ahlström Foundation.

Structure of giving

Type of Structure
The Eva Ahlström Foundation's financial resources come from individual family members and/or the family businesses. We receive no significant external funding. The foundation has, since March 2020, employed a part time assistant, but other than that the foundation and all subgroups are run by family members who volunteer their time and skills. We have a set of criteria in place that define the skills needed to join the board of the foundation.

Family Governance/Decision-Making
The foundation's board presents the work of the foundation at an annual family day at our traditional family residence. Initially, the foundation's board made annual financial requests to the family and business. Today, the foundation is independent, but donations are still welcome. To start the foundation, the 25 women from the family contributed with financial resources and, over time, the foundation's assets grew from an initial 25,000 EUR in 2010 to 5.1 million in 2019.

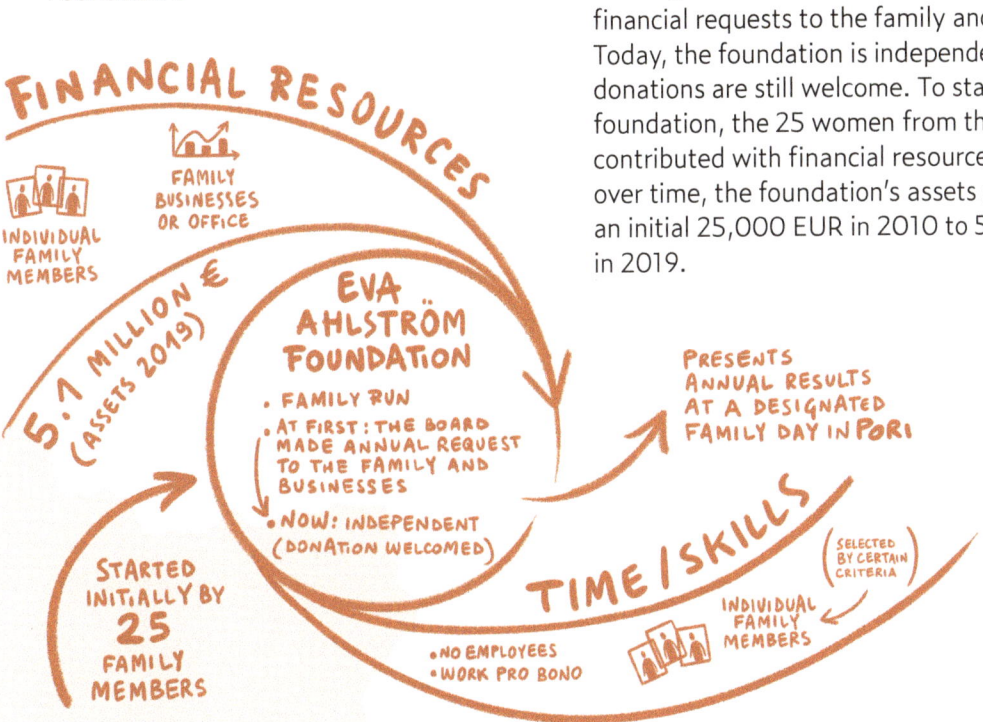

FINANCIAL RESOURCES
- INDIVIDUAL FAMILY MEMBERS
- FAMILY BUSINESSES OR OFFICE
- 5.1 MILLION € (ASSETS 2019)
- STARTED INITIALLY BY 25 FAMILY MEMBERS

EVA AHLSTRÖM FOUNDATION
- FAMILY RUN
- AT FIRST: THE BOARD MADE ANNUAL REQUEST TO THE FAMILY AND BUSINESSES
- NOW: INDEPENDENT (DONATION WELCOMED)

PRESENTS ANNUAL RESULTS AT A DESIGNATED FAMILY DAY IN PORI

TIME/SKILLS
- NO EMPLOYEES
- WORK PRO BONO
- INDIVIDUAL FAMILY MEMBERS (SELECTED BY CERTAIN CRITERIA)

Case Studies 69

Purpose

Navigator Questions

Motivation

→ **What inspires us to give? What drives us to give now or continue giving?**

Our ancestors Eva and Antti Ahlström championed women's equal right to education as well as a law that allowed women to inherit, and in various ways supported the communities in Finland where they had businesses.

Over time, the family became less engaged in direct giving as the government and taxation took on an increasingly important role in tackling local issues such as education and healthcare. However, as the business became international and entered emerging, lower wage markets, we started challenging our role in society to see how we could support local communities wherever we are active.

In 2010, we created the Eva Ahlström Foundation. The foundation made it possible for family members to be engaged and contribute to the family without having to be involved in the business. It became a platform for all family members to feel a part of something greater than themselves and contribute to the family's legacy in a meaningful way.

Focus

→ **What causes are we passionate about? In which regions do we give/want to give? Who or what ultimately benefits from our giving?**

We support underprivileged women, children and families in Finland and internationally. We have taken a strategic decision to work as a funding partner with recognized organizations as implementing partners. For example, UNICEF is our main partner.

Ambition

→ **What do we aim to achieve? What does success look like for us?**

We sincerely believe in doing "the right thing" according to universal values such as honesty, empathy, respect and justice. Our vision is to change the way "doing good" is perceived by advocating for compassion and action and strive to be the best version of ourselves.

We recognize that money alone will not solve the world's problems but a change in attitudes and structures goes a long way. We are very open to talking about philanthropy and sharing lessons learned with other philanthropists.

Success for us means building cohesion around our family, foundations, business, and giving. Recently, we launched an internationally recognized bold initiative called Ahlström Collective Impact in

KEY LEARNINGS AND RECOMMENDATIONS

1. **Communicate – a lot!** 25 women in the family started with a vision to improve the state of the world as a family. However, over time, we realized that in order to achieve this goal we had to communicate a lot more and a lot clearer with different members of the family if we wanted to engage them. Not doing this early on resulted in an artificial divide between "us" and "them." If you wish to engage your wider family, prepare a clear vision and communicate it often to different family members to ensure that they get equally excited and ultimately join your cause.

2. **Find your allies within the family.** As you are creating a network within the family, it's important that you identify "early adopters" or "allies" who believe in you and share your dream. Ideally, such a person will also enjoy a high level of respect from many family members, so that you can leverage him/her as a multiplier of your cause. It will take time and effort to create these ties, but it will most certainly pay off – for your family and, ultimately, for your cause.

3. **Aim at achieving a small success early on.** Start with small and humble, yet tangible and actionable, steps so that you can celebrate early successes. There's no value in pretending to solve all the world's problems in a massive mission statement. An early success, even if small, will help you gain trust and attention from the wider family.

4. **Create ownership.** Everyone wants to feel needed and to belong to something special. Give everyone a task and praise them for what they have done. A small contribution is a contribution towards something more meaningful. This is particularly relevant if you seek to work with family members only (most likely on a pro bono basis) and not hire any outside professionals.

5. **Find and leverage synergies.** When starting off, find a cause that brings everyone together or that everyone can relate to. Together, create something new from existing family values or history.

6. **Build the right team.** Your family is the A Team. Everyone is needed: the players on the field, the ones on the bench cheering you on, the older ones having played their part. You cannot score a goal alone. Appreciate and articulate team effort.

order to ensure that our various activities are aligned and that we, collectively, strive towards maximum positive impact. We aim to inspire our family, employees, customers, business partners and other stake holders to do the "right thing" according to universal values within our respective realities and lives.

We believe that this approach together with smart financial contributions to the right implementing partners, will make a real difference in the lives of vulnerable women and children.

Purpose

Case Study
The Tsao Ng Yu Shun Foundation
In Conversation with Dr Mary Ann Tsao

> "When one is clear about one's goals, everything else falls into place more easily".

- **Name:** Dr Mary Ann Tsao, Chair and Founding Director of the Tsao Ng Yu Shun Foundation, A family council member and director of The Tsao Family Office

- **Country of origin:** Family was originally from Shanghai, China. Dr Tsao's generation was born in Hong Kong, but she is currently based in Singapore.

- **Family size (total number of family members):** 4th gen: four members; 5th gen: five members; 6th gen: two members (primogeniture until 4th gen)

- **Background information about your family's legacy and current business activities:** We established our family business in the late 1800s in shipping and logistics. Our current family business also includes terminals and shipyards, real estate, hospitality and investments.

- **Which generation are you part of?** 4th generation

- **Number of family members involved in your philanthropic activities:** Four siblings from the 4th generation

Family Philanthropy Navigator

Areas of giving

Focus of Giving
We focus on issues of population aging, longevity and well-being of older people in an inclusive society.

Country/Region
We are active primarily in Singapore but at various times, we may have activities in Southeast Asia and South Asia.

Other Aspects Worth Noting
We aim to be a catalyst for constructive change, and we conduct research into emerging trends, pioneer solutions and engage in government policy advocacy to affect change.

Structure of giving

Type of Structure
We established the Tsao Foundation in 1992 in Singapore as an operational foundation. While we may give small grants to other organizations, we primarily run our own programs. Our family provides financial resources and the foundation's charitable services also generate revenues. The foundation also seeks external funding through government grants and subsidies.

Family Governance/Decision-Making
The foundation has its own board, but it has both family and independent directors. Four family members (from the fourth generation) are actively working in the family council and together make decisions about both the philanthropic activities of this foundation, other charitable giving as well as impact investing by the family office.

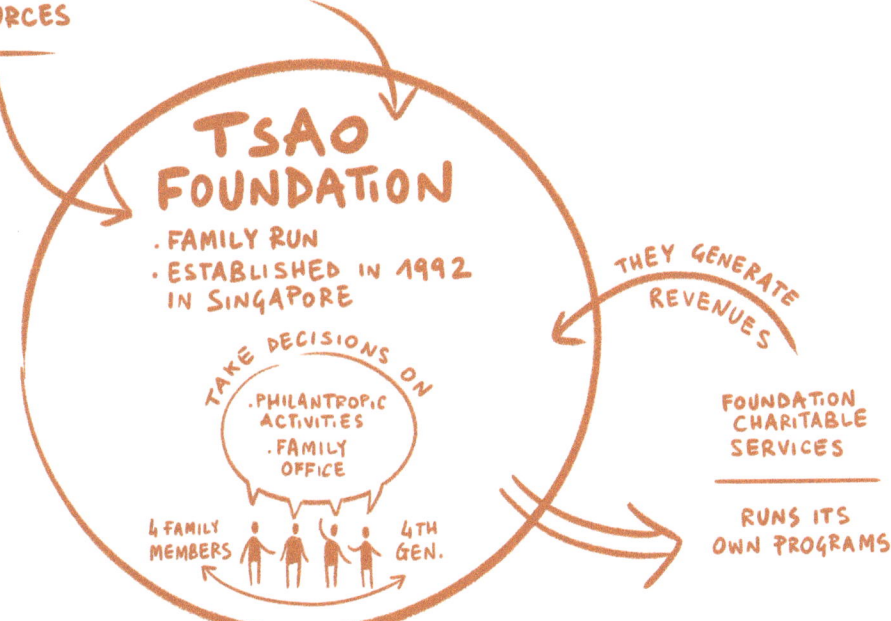

TSAO FAMILY PROVIDES FINANCIAL RESOURCES

GOVERNMENT GRANTS AND SUBSIDIES

TSAO FOUNDATION
- FAMILY RUN
- ESTABLISHED IN 1992 IN SINGAPORE

TAKE DECISIONS ON
- PHILANTROPIC ACTIVITIES
- FAMILY OFFICE

4 FAMILY MEMBERS   4TH GEN.

THEY GENERATE REVENUES

FOUNDATION CHARITABLE SERVICES

RUNS ITS OWN PROGRAMS

Case Studies

Purpose

Navigator Questions

Motivation

→ **What inspires us to give? What drives us to give now or continue giving?**

The foundation was the brainchild of my grandmother, Mrs Tsao Ng Yu Shun, and it has been led by me since the beginning in 1992.

My grandmother had several motives. First, she wanted to contribute to society in her own right and not just in her many roles as a daughter, sister, wife, mother and matriarch within the family. Second, she felt that modern society is unkind to old age and she wanted older people to have a better life and position in society. Finally, she wanted to create a legacy and a platform for her five children and the generations following, so that they and future family members would continue to be close because of their work together as trustees of the foundation.

What motivated me in the beginning was my commitment to my grandmother. Subsequently, after learning more about the situation of older people, I also wanted to address the social inequity and the gravity of the welfare situation for the elderly in Singapore.

Focus

→ **What causes are we passionate about? In which regions do we give/want to give? Who or what ultimately benefits from our giving?**

Our efforts focus on promoting and enabling aging in place by building a series of community-based demonstration service models (such as care management, home-based health care and end-of-life care) and advocating for national mainstreaming, inter-generational solidarity, capacity building, research, community development, as well as a systems and population approach to successful aging at the whole community level. We promote active aging for all, regardless of the state of physical health. Through our key initiatives – the Hua Mei Centre for Successful Ageing, the Hua Mei Training Academy, the International Longevity Centre Singapore and the Community for Successful Ageing – we are pioneering ways to empower mature adults to have self-determination over their own aging journeys in terms of self-care, growth and development.

We work primarily in Singapore, but increasingly our experience in Singapore has become a test bed for work in the Asia region, such as our current collaboration with the Asian Development Bank, which supports policy and practice development in long-term care in six Asian countries.

Ambition

→ **What do we aim to achieve? What does success look like for us?**
Through our effort, we hope to contribute not only to the well-being of older people, but to strengthen multi-generational family ties and community relations, as well as society's ability to reap the longevity dividend of the extra years of life. We want to have a positive impact on society with what we do and act as a lighthouse for others.

There are two main success factors:

1. We want to raise awareness of the challenges around aging and promote viable solutions at policy and practice levels, including ageing in place, successful ageing, as well as active aging (as defined by the World Health Organization) with a whole of community approach. We designed a whole blueprint for creating community-based services so elderly people can live comfortably at home. The more people we can touch with this, the better.
2. The foundation needs to be financially self-sustaining (not only accepting donations but also generating revenue). Therefore, we introduced some services and specialized training to generate revenue from fees.

KEY LEARNINGS AND RECOMMENDATIONS

1. **Have a clear purpose.** Clarity of purpose is essential. When one is clear about one's goals, everything else falls into place more easily. Even then, one may not achieve one's aims if the strategy, capability and resources are not appropriately deployed in implementation. But if one doesn't know where one is going, for sure, one is unlikely to get there.

2. **Become a catalyst for constructive change through excellence.** To be an effective catalyst, whatever one does must be excellent in order to have the desired impact. To create lasting change, one needs to show others that the proposed solution works - that what was seemingly impossible is actually possible. It is also important that one aims to inspire others in setting their own aspirations high and have the courage and confidence to persevere in order to realize the positive change they want to see for others.

3. **Gain financial sustainability.** Manage your funds responsibly – the inflow of your money has to match the obligations going out. Try to achieve a financially self-sustaining organization and generate additional revenue streams when possible.

4. **Run a healthy organization.** The success of your giving depends on how well-functioning your philanthropic organization is. Your staff, whether family or non-family, not only need to have their hearts in the right place and be committed to the cause, but they must also be competent and capable of delivering what is expected of them.

Case Studies

Purpose

Case Study
Fondation Juniclair

In Conversation with Marianne Ruggieri

"If you think you are too small to make a difference, try sleeping with a mosquito."

- **Name:** Ruggieri family

- **Country of origin:** France (based in Luxembourg)

- **Family size (total number of family members):** 2nd generation, three siblings and two parents.

- **Background information about your family's legacy and current business activities:** Batipart was founded in 1988 by Charles Ruggieri. The business started in real estate and, later, the family diversified their activities into healthcare, tourism and the hotel business. Today, the group is active in Europe, North America and Africa. In 2018, the management of the Batipart Group was passed down to the 2nd generation – the three children of Marianne and Charles Ruggieri.

- **Which generation are you part of?** 1st generation

- **Number of family members involved in your philanthropic activities:** Five family members (two from the 1st generation and three from the 2nd generation).

Family Philanthropy Navigator

Areas of giving

Focus of Giving
We support various development aid projects in the fields of education and the environment. We also work to support women in difficulty who are marginalized and/or subject to violence of any kind.

Country/Region
We are currently or have been active in countries in Asia, the Middle East, Africa, South America and Europe.

Structure of giving

Type of Structure
Juniclair (Julien, Nicolas and Claire) was founded in 2007 as an association. It was then re-organized as a public interest foundation in 2013. Formally, the foundation operates from Luxembourg.

Family Governance/Decision-Making
The Batipart holding company consists of five divisions: healthcare, tourism, real estate, hotel business and the foundation. The foundation's sole source of funding is the family holding company. The Batipart Group's annual contribution to Juniclair is approximately EUR one million. Batipart's philosophy is that its prosperity and sustainability are built on a solid bedrock of shared moral values.

2013 RE-ORGANIZED AS A PUBLIC INTEREST FOUNDATION

2007 FOUNDED AS AN ASSOCIATION

JUNICLAIR FONDATION — JULIEN NICOLAS CLAIRE

FAMILY FUNDING AND EXTERNAL CONTRIBUTIONS

1 MILLION EUROS PER YEAR

BATIPART HOLDING COMPANY
• FIVE DIVISIONS

HEALTH CARE · TOURISM · REAL ESTATE · HOTEL BUSINESS

SHARED MORAL VALUES

Case Studies 77

Purpose

Navigator Questions

Motivation

→ **What inspires us to give? What drives us to give now or continue giving?**
The initial motivation to create Juniclair was to pass our family values on to the next generation, as well as, to bring family members together. The project came to fruition following the birth of Marianne and Charles Ruggieri's grandchildren (the third generation) and was envisioned as a way of teaching them the importance of sharing one's economic success with those who have not been as fortunate.

The motivation is twofold. First, we want to make a difference and we want to see that our giving has a tangible impact. Second, we want to educate our younger generation about the importance of giving – and of doing so "the right way."

Focus

→ **What causes are we passionate about? In which regions do we give/want to give? Who or what ultimately benefits from our giving?**
We are very interested in making a difference in the fields of education and the environment. We also focus on empowering and working with women from all backgrounds who face hardships, such as being marginalized in society or the victims of violence and abuse. Marianne Ruggieri's experience and empathy for vulnerable children and their families was an important factor when it came to select the causes that we support.

We opt to make grants to not so well-known local charitable organizations that are often overlooked by traditional philanthropic institutions. We seek to cultivate long-term relationships with all the organizations that we fund, and to provide them with well-defined ongoing support, while taking into account the varying context of each collaboration.

Ambition

→ **What do we aim to achieve? What does success look like for us?**
We aim to make a significant, long-term difference for beneficiaries, with special attention to "people that history has left behind" and those who do not have the same opportunities as we have had in our societies. We provide high quality and customized support. We try to create and maintain deep, meaningful relationships with our beneficiaries.

The following principles are key elements of success for us:

→ To be and remain humble about how much we can help.
→ To do good, do it well, and do it discreetly.
→ To set high standards for impact, but also to be sensitive to the fact that circumstances often change.

KEY LEARNINGS AND RECOMMENDATIONS

1. **Define your impact and how you measure it.** Measuring impact should not be an objective but a central tool helping you to build and maintain effective collaborations. The only time a project we supported didn't work out in the way we had hoped was when we hadn't spent enough time clarifying what impact we expected to achieve through our giving.

2. **Leverage philanthropy as a learning mechanism.** The foundation has been a fantastic window into the world. Our family is active in a lot of different areas and philanthropy has really enabled us to discover what it means to be human, in all its greatness and simplicity and to explore the world – together.

3. **Purpose comes first.** It's essential to start by defining why you want to give, before making a more structured commitment. This process will take time, and you will need to let your ideas ripen before sharing them with other family members, and before you actually get started with your philanthropic activities.

4. **Set an example to the next generation.** We believe that it's important to share one's wealth and to set an example for the next generation. You are a role model to the youngsters, and they will learn from your actions.

5. **Let the younger generation define their own purpose of giving and support their journey.** Accept that each generation will want to redefine how they engage with the foundation and that they might want to adjust the course of action, including the purpose of their giving. Also, be there to support them in defining their own philanthropic journey.

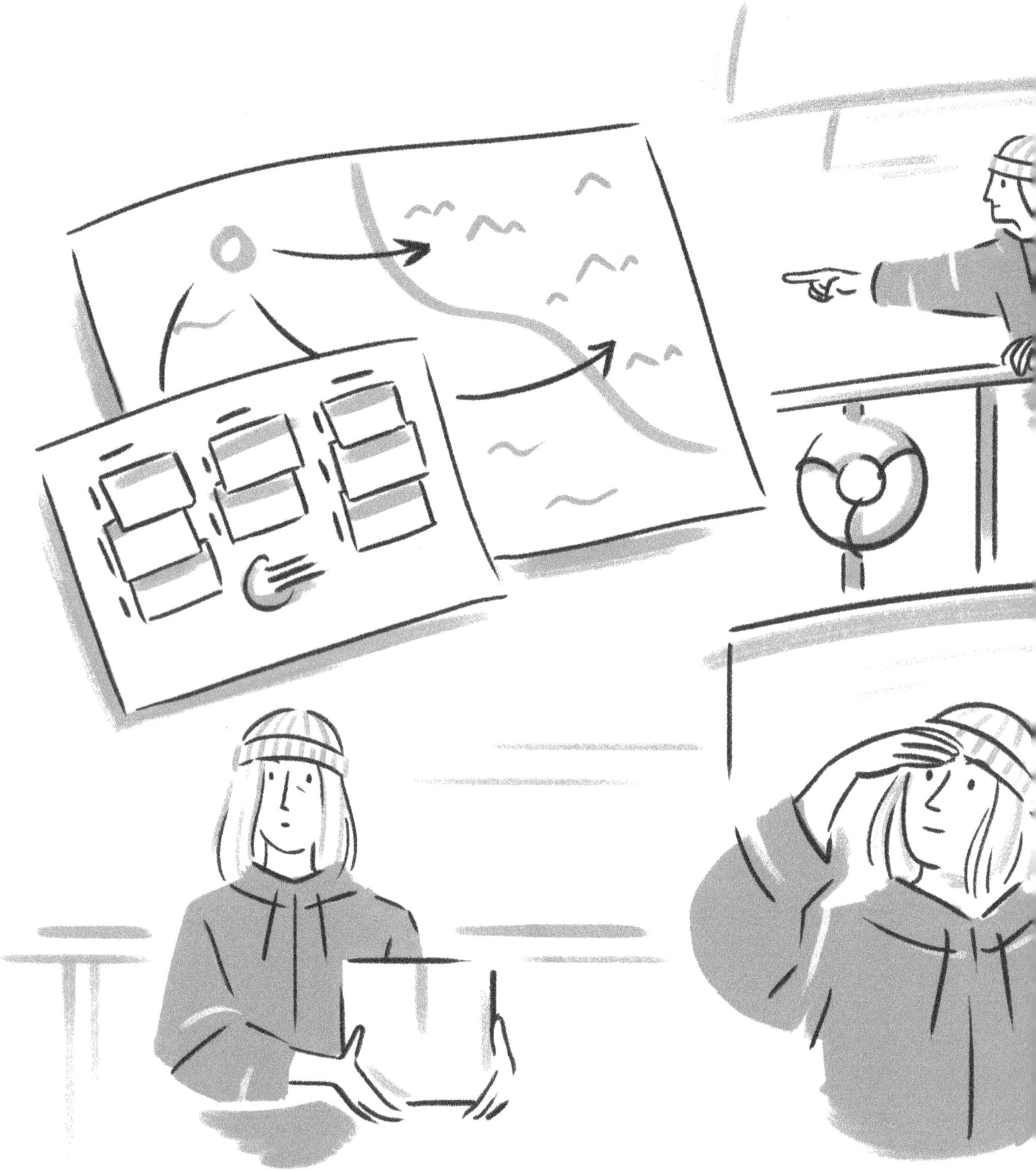

Relationships

88 **Family Involvement**

102 **Partners**

120 **Case Studies**

Relationships

Introduction

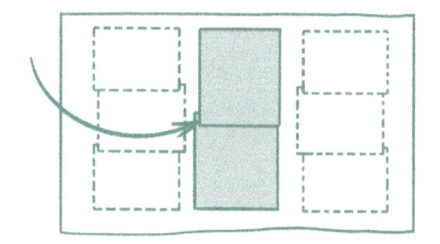

Who do you need to activate your giving and bring your ambitions to life? How will you involve your family and wider network? Will you work with lots of different partners or just a few? How will you decide who will be part of your philanthropic journey or team?

Philanthropy often starts as the idea of one, but it becomes the journey of many. No philanthropist is an island; effective giving cannot happen in a vacuum. Giving, like so many aspects of life, is about relationships: our friends and families, the organizations and experts we partner with to ensure that our resources are deployed effectively in the pursuit of our purpose. In philanthropy, success depends on the strength and health of the relationships between all actors involved. At the very least, giving requires a relationship between a donor and a recipient.

In reality, it calls for the proactive management of complex, intertwined relationships, within families and beyond.

Now that you have come to some meaningful conclusions about the purpose of your giving, it is time to build your team.

→ **For aspiring philanthropists**, in this step of the navigator, we will help you to explore and understand the ways in which your family and other partners can support your philanthropic journey.
→ **For more established philanthropists**, we will provide an opportunity to conduct a health check of your family and partner ecosystem and to consider any changes you might want to make to enhance how you work or if there has been a change of circumstances.

Ultimately, you will answer three key navigator questions to select your team and assign roles:

→ **Family involvement**: Who from our family is/will be involved? What is the nature of that involvement?

→ **Partners**: Who do we need or want to partner with, outside the family, in order to implement our giving?

It is important to take time to reflect on who need to be in your team to achieve your ambitions, and what roles they can or should play. This applies to both individuals as well as organizations.

Do you want to start and activate a philanthropic activity on your own or contribute to the work of an existing foundation or charitable organization? Do you want to draw on the talents and time of your immediate family to build or refine a family philanthropic journey? How do you manage their involvement? Will you need to work with other donors to achieve your aims? What type of professional partners do you need? What kind of relationship do you want to have with the recipient of your giving? Why do you need other partners? Surely, if you want to give funds to a specific cause, you can just go ahead and cut out the middlemen? This can be true when you start, of course, but there are compelling reasons to work with partners because, today, philanthropy demands as much professionalism and integrity as any other walk of life.

Many projects will require additional support from the outside. Strong partnerships in philanthropy create the conditions for a better start and sustainable results. Asking an experienced friend to sit on your foundation board, seeking expert help from an independent advisor, or working with an NGO that understands the terrain will strengthen your approach and increase the chances of achieving your ambitions.

Introduction

Relationships

Choosing the right relationships in philanthropy can also fill gaps in your knowledge, skills and experience. Bankers and lawyers can help with the financial and structural aspects of setting up a foundation or planning a series of grants over several years. Philanthropy advisors can help you learn from others or set off on your course in the right direction. Hiring experienced staff can help you to turn your ambitions into reality. Many family businesses are successful because of external help; philanthropy is no different.

Nonetheless, for most philanthropists, the immediate (or wider) family forms an integral part of the philanthropic journey. On the one hand, this is because many philanthropic families leverage philanthropy as a vehicle to engage relatives in the family enterprise system, especially if they are not directly involved in the business. Philanthropy can be a great way to nurture family cohesion and to fulfill a greater purpose together.

On the other hand, family resources are being used. In order to avoid any misunderstandings or conflicts of interest, it is advisable to inform and seek the approval in some form or other family members before you commit to any philanthropic action.

By the end of this section, you will have reflected on how to involve family members and other partners in your "ecosystem of giving."

This ecosystem will form the backbone of the structure and organization of your philanthropic activities, which will be explored further in the Organization section of the navigator. As a starting point, it is useful to map out your own personal ecosystem as suggested in this illustration.

Insight

SAVE 10% AND GIVE 10%

When families share wealth over generations, it can be challenging for the next generation to define its own identity in relation to their wealth. Therefore, in addition to developing professional skills to make a living, money should be saved and given to others, for example, based on the 10% principle where you retain 20% of your earnings to save 10% and to give 10% to philanthropic causes. In that way, as a member of the next generation, you can explore your own philanthropic passions and nurture your identity. Families that are successful over generations acknowledge the importance of every member of the next generation having to earn their own money, save and learn to give to others.

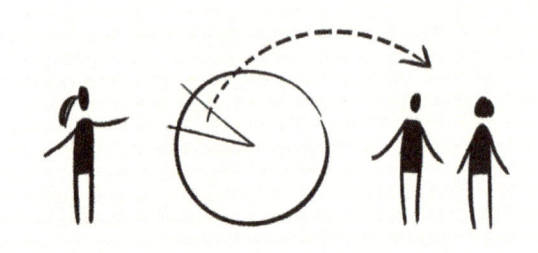

THE EVOLUTION OF YOUR PHILANTHROPY

STAGE 1
MY PHILANTHROPY
AS YOU START YOUR REFLECTION

ME AND MY PHILANTHROPY

STAGE 2
THE INITIAL ECOSYSTEM OF OUR PHILANTHROPY
AS YOU BUILD YOUR STRUCTURE

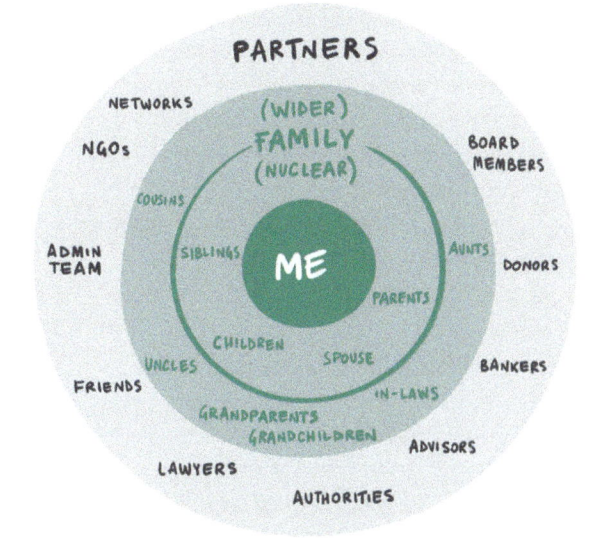

PARTNERS
- NETWORKS
- NGOs
- ADMIN TEAM
- FRIENDS
- LAWYERS
- AUTHORITIES
- ADVISORS
- BANKERS
- DONORS
- BOARD MEMBERS

(WIDER) FAMILY (NUCLEAR)
- COUSINS
- SIBLINGS
- UNCLES
- CHILDREN
- GRANDPARENTS / GRANDCHILDREN
- SPOUSE
- IN-LAWS
- PARENTS
- AUNTS
- ME

STAGE 3
AN INTEGRATED APPROACH FOR OUR FAMILY PHILANTHROPY
AS YOU PROGRESS IN YOUR PHILANTHROPY AS A FAMILY

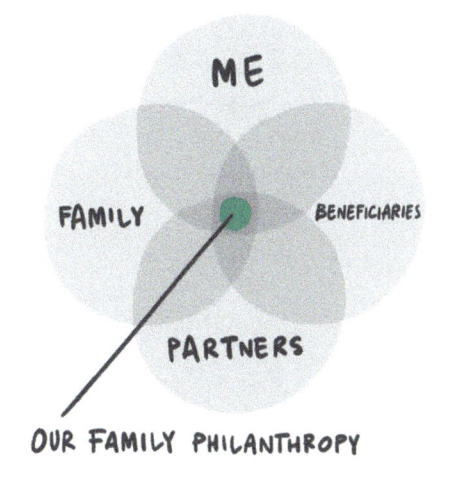

ME / FAMILY / BENEFICIARIES / PARTNERS

OUR FAMILY PHILANTHROPY

Introduction 85

Relationships

Depending on the scope of your ambitions and resources, you might prefer to keep things simple by working with only a few close family members and a couple of external partners. However, if you are establishing a foundation with significant funds and want to tap into wider family expertise and resources, it is likely that your philanthropic plans will demand the involvement of a larger number of actors.

Each of those relationships, within and outside of the family, then needs thoughtful, clear guidance and stewardship so that the whole machine operates smoothly. Governance will also become of critical importance as the complexity of the system increases, as we will explain in the next section.

As stated earlier, philanthropy is often the idea of one, but it becomes the journey of many. It is only natural that you start alone on this journey. However, philanthropy is, in essence, a movement and gesture from the self towards others, where everyone becomes a partner. The most effective philanthropy often features a strong ecosystem of partnerships, built on trust, respect and equality, where the whole becomes more important than the self.

We recommend that, over time, you conceive your philanthropic journey as a collaborative, learning journey. This process began in the Purpose section of this book, as you reflected on the motivation, focus and ambition of your and your family's giving.

In this section, we would like to invite you to explore how philanthropy is enriched by building clear, well-managed relationships within a fluid philanthropic ecosystem.

Family involvement

The first part of the Relationships section of our navigator focuses exclusively on family involvement. This is an important, and often sensitive, area that requires diplomacy as you make a careful assessment of which individuals from your family to involve, as well as how and why they will be involved. An open and well-communicated process is often the right approach to start, or to relaunch, such as a discussion in the family. Whatever your ambitions may be, this reflection is crucial in moving from purpose to activation. For the experienced philanthropist, it is an opportunity to revitalize your family through giving or to rethink how your family works together within philanthropy. This chapter also offers a chance to understand how to use philanthropy as a way to engage the next generation in the family enterprise system.

Partners

As a philanthropist, you will essentially have two families: your natural relatives and, then, a wider network of friends, peers, professionals and organizations whom you may need to help you structure and deliver your giving. The second part of the Relationships section focuses on helping you to identify the types of non-family partners you will need in order to bring your philanthropic vision to life. In this chapter, we will help you understand the options to complete your team. For experienced philanthropists, it is an opportunity to assess your current ecosystem and to consider any changes.

Introduction

Relationships

Family Involvement

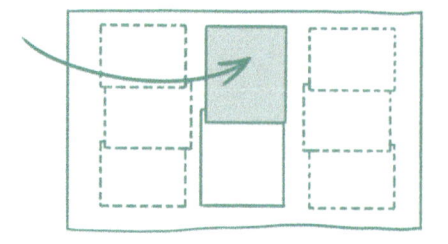

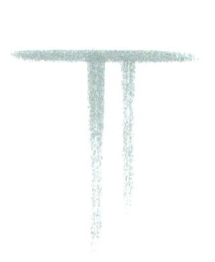

Setting the Scene

Successful, long-lasting families often think in generations, not in years. It is, therefore, useful to look at how "the family" has evolved over recent decades.

The notion of family has changed as our societies have changed. Fifty years ago, life for most of us was mainly localized to a limited geographical environment with perhaps 200 contacts within a community. Intergenerational solidarity was the norm. The notion of "self" was not central to societies.

Today, most of us live in a city, our community is the world and individualism often comes before family, with thousands of "friends" on social media. The aim is not just to become independent, but autonomous.

Consumerism is at the center of our lives: news, goods, holidays, relationships.

The family no longer holds the same sense of gravity for the next generation. The concept of family has transformed from being close to your relatives to being close to like-minded individuals from around the world. As a result, we see the rise of "tribes" and communities all over the world, which particularly attracts Millennials and digital natives, as they seek a secure base and a sense of belonging. At the same time, the next generation faces a new reality where they are expected (either by their peers or by themselves) to tick off all items on their bucket list, which can compromise their time for contemplation and being guided by great principles. Younger people are hungry for inspiration and beacons in a world often marked by uncertainty and anxiety.

Although generosity has always existed, there is a growing opportunity today to embrace and develop it within families

Family Philanthropy Navigator

more proactively or explicitly. Generations are eager to create new space for meaningful conversations and collaboration. Philanthropy can become a platform to nurture the family through moments of truth and wisdom; it teaches generosity, allows for the transmission of values and beliefs, and emphasizes the meaning and importance of others.

The relationship between parents and children is changing. We might also be witnessing a shift from a model of assistance to a model of reciprocity within families. Members of the next generation are becoming more independent from the senior generation and are taking more ownership of what they want to take responsibility for.

In this paradigm, families can be seen as a great source of expertise, ideas, talent, energy and experience. Bringing in relatives from your wider family opens up a pool of resources, but can also trigger other challenges, from governance and conflict resolution to communication and administration. Getting the balance right between close family members and other relatives can be an important topic on its own.

Nurturing your family should not be the sole reason for family philanthropy. But philanthropy can be beneficial to the long-term health of the family ecosystem as a neutral platform and safety valve for communication and collaboration, as well as for embracing the diversity of views and principles within the family. This step of the navigator will equip you with the necessary tools to examine whom from your family you would like or need to involve in order to achieve your ambitions, both in philanthropy and as a family.

Ultimately, it will enable you to answer the following navigator questions:

→ Who from our family is/will be involved? What is the nature of that involvement?

Family Involvement

Relationships

→ If the purpose of your giving includes a focus on family, for example, then you may need to consider how you can achieve that in practice through specific and structured family involvement. This step will also begin the process of thinking about roles and resources – not just whom you need from your family, but what they can bring to the table and what gaps remain that must then be filled by external partners.

You will find further guidance and support for making these choices in the Resources chapter of the Organization section of this book, where you will be able to conduct a thorough assessment of the resources you have at hand and the gaps you need to fill.

Insight

ENGAGE THE NEXT GENERATION EARLY

Philanthropy lies at the crossroads of family dynamics and money. It is not always easy to get an initial, straightforward impetus or connection between donors and their next generation members. Here are some practical tips on the many ways to engage the next generation effectively:

Young children
→ Start discussing the causes you care about with your children when they are young, as well as the service you do for society and your favorite way of giving.
→ Pocket money should initially be a way to "experience" money. The Rockefeller family developed the notion of the three-part allowance, the "3 S's" for pocket money with an equal weight between spending, saving and sharing.
→ Children are inspired by behavior: tell them about your family rituals, and volunteer.

Adolescents
→ Talk about the meaning of money.
→ Encourage peer activities at school, or during summer camps.
→ Involve them in site visits to meet with giving partners or to see what you support.
→ Explore creating a grandchildren's fund to add a conversation beyond your own generation.
→ If you have a family fund/foundation, involve them informally in the board or conversations to make these activities feel tangible and "real."

College age and young adults
→ Create funds matching their own gifts to support their nascent endeavors.
→ Develop with your family foundation discretionary grant making (that is, give your family members a portion of funds to donate as individuals) so that they can explore their own responsibilities in giving.
→ Encourage and support apprenticeships during vacations or free time as well as training.
→ Reflect on including them via an adjunct/next generation foundation board so that they can explore philanthropy among themselves.

Adult "children"
→ Be transparent about the process and requirements for becoming full trustees.
→ Share with them official foundation documents such as donor intent and bylaws.

Setting the Compass

Before settling on the best way to harness the potential within your family, the following trade-offs will help to inform your reflections and choices. Take some time to think about the different ways you can combine the options on offer to best achieve your goals, as a philanthropist but also as a member of a family. Bear in mind your conclusions from the Purpose section of this book. For example, if one of your core motivations is to unite the family, educate and onboard the next generation, you should embrace a more inclusive approach when it comes to involving other family members.

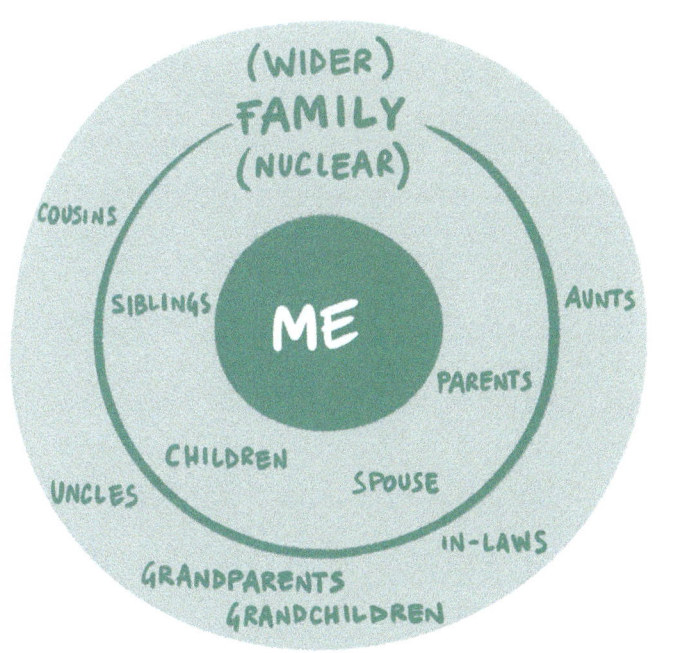

INDIVIDUAL VS NUCLEAR FAMILY VS WIDER FAMILY

Families differ in size, complexity and dynamics, and it follows that there are many ways to involve family members in philanthropy. Deciding which family members to involve – and in what manner – begins with a reflection of what your own role will be, before considering if members of your immediate or nuclear family can and should be involved, followed by your wider family. This process can be complicated, requiring careful diplomacy, clarity and foresight.

→ Do you want to give **on your own**?
→ Do you want to **include** your nuclear family only or **spread** the net wider?
→ Are there **specific** branches of the family you want to **engage** with?
→ Do you want to **combine** the resources of a range of members from the **wider family** with **varying** levels of **responsibility** and in **different roles**?
→ Will you include **in-laws** or **children** from later marriages?

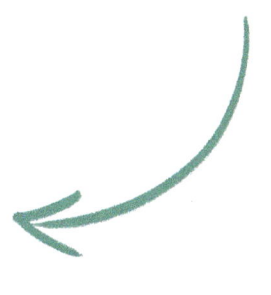

Family Involvement 91

Relationships

SINGLE GENERATION ———————————— **MULTIPLE GENERATIONS**

Engage only one generation in your giving

Family philanthropy can focus primarily on the close-knit activity of siblings, or it can stretch to include engagement across several generations, perhaps as a way to build unity, onboard the next generation or transfer values. Either approach – and any iteration in between – has its strengths and weaknesses, and also ties back to the purpose of your giving. For example, engaging several generations can require an awareness of the diverse past experiences and perspectives that exist between older and younger members of your family.

Engage two or more generations in your giving

→ Are you interested in working only with your **siblings** or **cousins**, perhaps to **build bonds** or **pursue common interests**?
→ Do you want to **empower** the next generation, pass on certain values or **embrace philanthropy** as a way to **onboard** relatives into the family enterprise system?
→ Has there been a change of **family leadership** or circumstances that requires **rethinking** who is involved?
→ Do you have new ambitions for a **close-knit project** to involve the next generations?

NOTES

_____

_____

_____

Family Philanthropy Navigator

HANDS ON ├─┼─┼─┼──┼──┼─┼─┼─┤ **HANDS OFF**

Being closely involved in leading your philanthropic activities

For each family member, it is important to clarify the exact nature of philanthropic involvement. This can range from the entire adventure being operationally "hands-off," where you and your family set the focus and ambitions for your giving but then outsource the rest to external partners or hire professional employers. At the other end of the spectrum, the family might want to be intensely involved in the management of every step of the process and get truly "hands-on" on the ground. There is clearly a myriad of options in between – and the best balance will depend on the specific expectations and needs of your family. Many enterprising families balance their involvement between the two, engaging where they can while hiring advisors to guide them and partners to implement their giving in concrete projects.

Delegate operational activities in your giving to others

→ How **hands-on** or **hands-off** do you want to, or can you and your family, be in your giving?
→ Do you want to **select** a handful of family members for **key, "hands-on" roles**, while asking others to take more of a **back seat**?
→ Do your family **want** to be involved?
→ What **level of engagement** do you expect from your family members?
→ What **roles** do your family members **want to play**?

NOTES

_____

_____

_____

Family Involvement

Relationships

BLOODLINE FIRST ⊢┼┼┼┼┼┼┼┼┤ COMPETENCY FIRST

Access and right to involvement based on being a (bloodline) descendent of the founder

If you wish your philanthropy to be both family controlled and family run, then the question of legitimacy, access and responsibilities might grow as the family grows and generations pass. This can either mean only allowing bloodline relatives to be part of your philanthropic journey, or allowing involvement purely on professional qualifications and expertise, or it could mean a mixed approach. As you don't – legally speaking – own a foundation that serves the public interest, it might be helpful and relevant to reflect on the core principles that you want to adopt regarding your family's involvement and, especially, spouses. Principles can change, but it is important to continue to reflect over time on where the talent and the engagement comes from.

Access and right to involvement is based on qualifications, achievements and capabilities

→ Will legitimacy, access or the right to be involved and make decisions depend on whether or not family members are **direct descendants** of the founders?
→ Will you only base involvement decisions on **professional skills** and **qualifications**?
→ If the family grows, how will the various **competences** and **experiences** of family members be **harnessed** and **managed**?
→ Will you **combine** the **two approaches** in some way?

NOTES

_____

_____

_____

94 Family Philanthropy Navigator

Good Practice in Creating a Family Culture of Giving

Motivations for giving can vary, as we have seen, from a sense of responsibility ("to whom much is given, much is expected") to a sense of joy. It is important to encourage family members to reflect on their personal passions, interests and concerns, so that they can enjoy philanthropy and foster a culture of giving across generations. Here are some helpful "best practice" tips for the different generations.

Legitimate Betrayals
There can be a tension between the legacy of the senior generation and the innovative ideas of the next generation. Recognize that the next generation may want to build its own individual and collective identity while also balancing the instinct or pressure to align with the family's code and activities. Members of the next generation will develop their own personalities that could result in diverging views. In the process of transferring a philanthropic journey, the senior generation needs to acknowledge that the next generation may want to do things differently.

New Platform for Generational Bonding
As in any family, the period of generational transition offers both a perspective and a lament. The relationships between children and their parents and the relationships between siblings are not built on the same basis. For the latter, the governing principle is one of sharing. This relationship between siblings needs to be developed by choices and discovering mutual interest. Philanthropy can offer a new space for families to engage across generations, and occasionally express disagreement in a relatively "neutral" space.

Inspire Kindness and Lead by Example
Across generations, try to inspire each generation to be kind to each other and to others. Members of the next generation tend to copy the behavior of their role models rather than automatically adopt "written" values that may not be practiced by the senior generation. Therefore, parents need to lead by example: to walk the talk to ensure credibility, and to inspire their children to follow suit.

Create Space and Time for Storytelling
Legacy is a powerful motivator. The sense of legacy comes from the senior generation. Predecessors can be a great source of inspiration because of what they have achieved over their lifetimes. It is important to record and celebrate other family members' engagement and to cultivate a family-conscious history. With new media and technology, there is now a new range of ways to do this.

Family Involvement

Let's Talk Money

Philanthropy involves a transfer of funds from within a family to external causes and partners. For family members, this can have knock-on effects in areas such as inheritance and scope for current investment. Before embarking on any philanthropic journey, or when you involve new members of the family, discuss financial matters openly with all family members affected by the decision. This increases engagement and clears the air to avoid any future disagreements or confusion. In that sense, philanthropy can help build conversations around who gets what, and to what end.

Communicate with Clarity and Facilitate Engagement

Philanthropic progress and endeavors should be accessible and transparent to other family members (e.g. through family retreats, family intranet, impact stories). It also makes sense to have activities for "less involved" family members to better understand the philanthropy journey, such as testimonials and field visits. Clear communication from the start about decision-making, roles and responsibilities, expectations and ambitions will set the tone for what follows, just as in any professional environment. This can be even more relevant for families, where other relationship dynamics come into play.

Insight

WHAT THE NEXTGEN HAS TO SAY OR WOULD LIKE TO SAY

Communicating within families is a challenge in the context of philanthropy. The following testimonials share the experiences of a group of next generation family members, who are part of a peer group discussion that we regularly facilitate, in their dealings with senior generations:

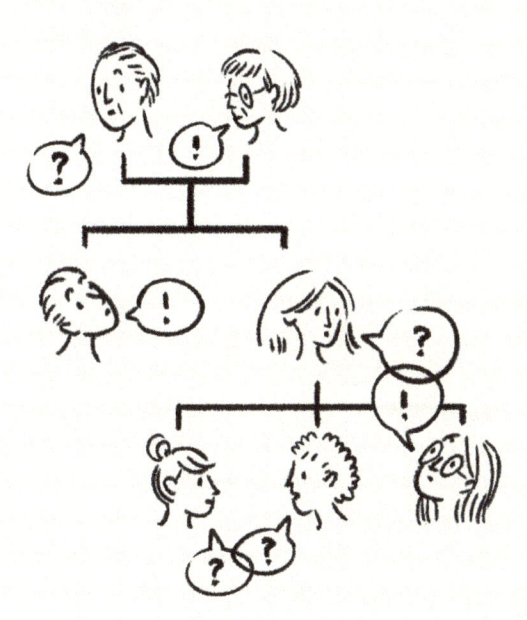

→ **What do we want to learn from our family philanthropy?**
Best practices, diplomacy, learning perspectives, experience, diversity of opinions, entrepreneurship, patience, respect, credibility, networks, legacy, greater sense of purpose, values, professional connections, family bonding.

→ **What do we want to bring to our family philanthropy?**
Innovation, creativity, change, education, perspectives, vision, passion, uniting the family, structure for the NextGen, Millennial ideas, focus and growth.

→ **What do we want to hear from our parents?**
Acceptance, openness, trust, encouragement, autonomy, support, values, be the change, communication.

→ **What do we want to say to our parents?**
Show interest in current projects, be involved, tell us your stories to inspire us, collaboration, trust, include us, empower us, but please do not hinder, have faith in us, authority vs autonomy, try to understand the world we live in.

Family Involvement

Relationships

Activities

You have now explored the themes and factors that will help you shape your decisions when it comes to involving your family in your philanthropy. The following activities will help you refine and choose your preferences. If you are new to philanthropy, this will mean making some decisions about which family members to involve and how. If you are more experienced, it's time to take stock and reassess your current setup.

Family Philanthropy Navigator Questions:

→ Who from our family is/will be involved?
→ What is the nature of that involvement?

Activity 1:
Review Your Trade-Offs

Step 1

Review the trade-offs presented earlier in this chapter and, individually, answer the following questions. Use different colors to visually highlight the two questions in each of the trade-offs. You can position yourself anywhere along the spectrum from one end to the other end of the trade-off.

1. **Where is our philanthropy today?**
2. **Where would I like our philanthropy to be in the future?**

Step 2

As a family, compare and discuss where each one of you positioned the dots for "where are we today" and "where would we like to be". What are the similarities and differences? Where are you aligned or not? How can this further shape your journey?

Step 3

If there are any differences in your perspectives, discuss how you wish to address these.

* Note to aspiring philanthropists:
If you are not yet philanthropically active you can simply focus on question 2 in Step 1.

Family Involvement

Relationships

Activity 2: Building Your Philanthropy Tribe

Now that you have worked through some of the options available to you. It is time to sketch out the blueprint for your family's involvement in your philanthropic journey. The following exercises will help you to experiment and narrow down choices and, ultimately, to answer the key navigator questions for this section.

Step 1

Identify People
Individually, fill in the table. Use this graphic to identify members of your family you want to work with, or you think would need to be informed about your philanthropic journey. At this stage, reflect mainly on your family network in relation to the ambition of your project.

Usually one of the core reflections is to decide whether you involve close relatives only, such as your children, spouse, siblings and parents (first circle), or also reach into the wider family nucleus. The latter might involve uncles, aunts, in-laws and cousins (second circle).

NAME

Branch/generation/etc.
Who are they? What role do they play in the family?

Contribution to your journey
How could they support your philanthropy?

Expectations
What might be their expectations from being part of this philanthropic journey?

Roles
What formal or informal role(s) could they play?

Step 2

Build the Initial Crew of Your Ship

Start sketching the roles that each person can or could fulfill, while also reflecting on their contribution and expectations. Continue forming your answers using the remaining rows of the same table.

It will be helpful to conduct this exercise as a group but, first, we recommend that you explore the possibilities on your own.

Should you decide to do it as a group, it is important to have one person in charge of the process who facilitates the conversation. This can be someone from the family or an independent person. We recommend that you do not play this role yourself so that you can be free to participate fully.

An alternative is to lead each conversation separately and then consolidate the results. You might then need an independent person to help you, as this is a lengthier process.

Step 3

Consolidate

Consolidate a complete table. Reflect, individually, and as a group, on how you could manage the expectations raised by your family. Outline clearly to all family members that you have involved or that you think might need to be informed what can and cannot be done. Finally, agree a way forward with roles and responsibilities.

Remember that clear communication, as well as a clear process are key factors to progress in this exercise, and in your philanthropy.

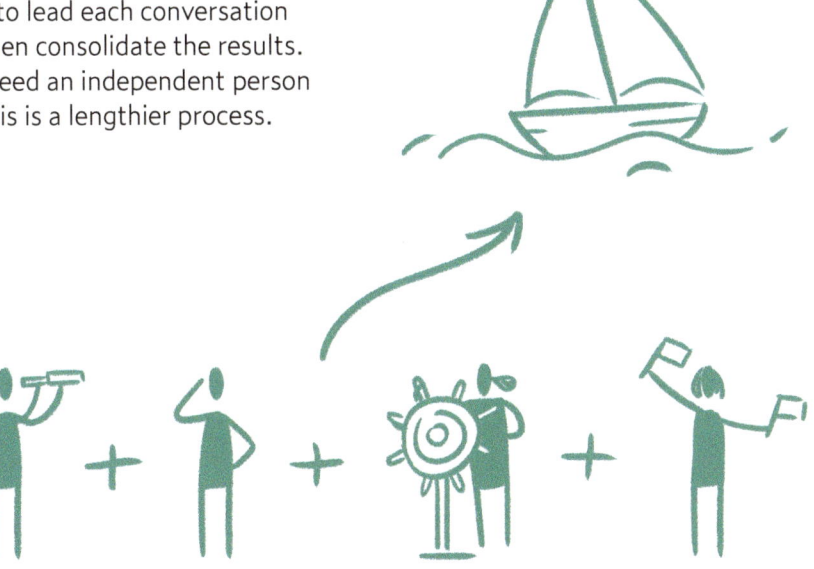

Family Involvement 101

Relationships

Partners

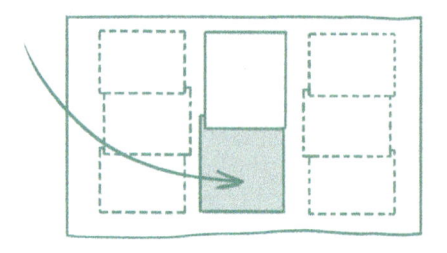

Setting the Scene

In an increasingly interconnected and complex world, it is highly likely that you will need to venture beyond the realms of your family to deliver on your ambitions in philanthropy.

External partners can fill gaps in skills and resources, bring valuable experience and knowledge, and they can also provide much needed perspective and guidance. These partners range from external board members in a foundation right through to the final recipient of your giving. In fact, philanthropy only becomes a reality when projects, organizations or their leaders are supported financially or through other means by partners. We will elaborate on how this works in the Organization section of this book.

Selecting partners outside of the family is an important decision and a delicate process that should be based on a careful assessment of your needs, the scope of your ambitions and the degree of professionalism you want. As you now know what you want to achieve and the resources within your own family, it is time to define what other people and organizations you need to engage with and how. We suggest that you aim to involve two main groups of partners.

Partners as Your Advisors

Here we mean philanthropy advisors, legal counsel, financial experts, educators, employees, or even possibly board members. They are your "backroom team". Within the ecosystem of giving, there is a vibrant range of "non-family" partners that can support you as you make decisions, build structures and implement your giving. It is unlikely that you will need all of them all of the time, or perhaps even most of the time. Some of them may be heavily involved, others may be more distant or absent, or only involved at a certain stage of your journey. These kinds of partners will help you in governing your foundation, choosing the right structure, achieving greater impact, facilitating collaboration across generations, and so on.

The following key questions will guide your initial reflections:

1. What other skills, experience and knowledge do you need in order to deliver on your purpose?
2. Who can help you to work towards your philanthropic goals?
3. How will you go about selecting them?

You might want also to consider where exactly you could include partners in your philanthropy:

→ **Board members, advisory board members.** You might want to include advisors within the governing body of your structure. Usually, these commitments are longer term and, most of the time, pro bono in philanthropy, or for minimal fees.

→ **External advisors.** You might want to gain ad hoc support from third parties for a specific task (such as legal advisory, strategic advisory, NextGen engagement, education) or longer term to ensure and build a process (such as asset management). In general, these relationships are based on a contract or mandate.

→ **Employees.** Depending on the size of your operations, or the need for specific expertise, you may consider hiring people within your structure to deliver some of the tasks of your philanthropy endeavor.

Relationships

→ **Networks.** Be it formal (such as membership of an association) or informal (such as working groups, peers, other foundations), you might want to consider involving important, existing actors within the field of your giving.

Partners as Philanthropic Counterpart

You will also need to choose a partner that will be the "hands-on" final recipient of your giving and that will be active and effective in delivering your ambitions on the ground. This choice – and the relationship involved – is a critical one, whether it is an NGO, a charity, a social enterprise or even if you give directly to an individual, a school, a hospital or an art gallery. However, when shaping this central partnership to your giving, it might also be useful to work with an advisor or peer donor to leverage their experience and expertise. If you plan a larger endeavor, hiring professionals to work for you should be seriously considered.

The following key questions will guide your initial reflection:

1. What kind of organization would I like to support? (e.g. **an international NGO, large well-known charity, small local charity, social enterprise**)?
2. How will I go about identifying them?
3. What will my selection criteria be to engage with them?
4. How will I engage with them throughout the process?

Later in this chapter, we will also offer a list of giving principles to facilitate healthy relationships with the partners you work with and give grants to.

It is important that you take the necessary time to reflect on the different options you have and learn from best practice examples (e.g. from other families with similar ambitions). This will help you bring clarity and structure to whom you would like to or need to partner with in order to achieve your philanthropic goals. This chapter of the navigator will assist you in identifying which "non-family" partners will help you to deliver on your vision. By the end of this chapter, you should be able to answer the following guiding question:

→ Who do we need or want to partner with, outside the family, in order to implement our giving?

Insight

Partners in Giving

There are many reasons to seek the support of external partners in philanthropy. Here you will find a brief description of some of these players, and how they might fit into your giving ecosystem. It may be helpful, at this stage, to cross reference with the Resources chapter in the Organization section as you reflect on the competences you might need to fill gaps in your existing pool of family members.

→ **Thematic expertise:** As you develop a strategy for your giving, you might need experts that can help you with funding decisions or to identify how to best address specific issues. Over time, the partners you fund will provide you with insights, but it is always helpful to access expertise and guidance closer to your governing body. Such experts can either act as outside advisors, or join you in a more formal role, such as on your foundation board.

→ **Legal advice:** Setting up your structure, reporting to authorities and formalizing contracts with grantees and suppliers are all important tasks for any foundation. Lawyers and foundation associations can provide resources to tackle these elements. Alternatively, peer donors and philanthropy advisors can assist to shape your grant making.

→ **Financial advice:** Traditionally, bankers have played this role. It is important to consider, for example, whether they are able to advise you via your board and also manage your assets, both liquid and illiquid. For practical reasons, you might want to separate these roles. In addition, there are numerous independent financial advisors with expertise in impact investing and sustainable finance. For larger families, a family office can provide financial advice.

→ **Facilitation or moderation of family conversations:** A family foundation, led by a family, often benefits from having a neutral party to facilitate conversations. Any collaboration among multiple family members and across generations might involve sensitive issues. A third pair of eyes can help to ensure creative continuity.

→ **External evaluation or continuous education:** In a rapidly changing world, where it is often hard to make time, stepping back to reflect on one's impact is an important part of the learning we advocate within our navigator. External evaluators can provide help with an assessment of your impact. Continuous education can help in gaining new perspectives, acquire new knowledge or arrive at a common understanding for all parties.

Relationships

Setting the Compass

As you begin to explore and understand your needs and the options you have in terms of possible partners, the following trade-offs will help you frame your thinking and to simplify the choices that lie ahead. Do you want to work with anyone outside of your family? How do you want to interact with intermediaries? Who are the best possible partners to achieve our goals?

It is worth recalling the choices you made in the Purpose section as you work through these reflections.

Here we present some of the trade-offs that you will face while building or maintaining your support network.

Insight

MANAGE CONFLICTS OF INTEREST

While we need different types of relationships with varied partners to realize our vision for giving, it is worth keeping an open mind about any competing interests within that ecosystem. For example, a banker managing your funds and sitting on your board might prefer a long-term foundation model and gradual plan for your giving, while you and your family might want to move at a faster, more flexible pace. There may be a family member who might want to be involved and, at the same time, sit on the board of charities you are supporting. First, you should ask yourself: Are these one-off blockages or are they recurrent conflicts? Then, consider ways to mitigate those conflicts to avoid any lasting disruption, perhaps by establishing clear governance structures and processes within your ecosystem.

We recommend, in general:

1. Asking partners you work with to openly declare any possible conflicts of interest.

2. Should there be a recurring conflict of interest, you might wish to regulate it in a written format.

3. Review the situation annually to make sure you are on track.

REACTIVE ——|——|——|——|——|——|——|——|——|—— **PROACTIVE**

Exclusively reacting to incoming proposals from NGOs/charities/social enterprises

Consider whether you want to receive proposals as a reactive philanthropist or reach out to partners, perhaps via a call for proposals or the support of professionals, as a proactive philanthropist, or whether you want to adopt a blended or ad hoc approach. It is important to clarify these choices because they will shape how you build and maintain key partnerships. If you want to be more reactive, prepare a profile of the kind of partner you are looking for, share the process for review and then respond to solicitations. This implies a greater ability to make approvals, refusals or request revisions. If you choose to be more proactive, conduct research and due diligence and engage with experts to understand who can help you fulfill your purpose. This implies a greater ability to understand the field you are in.

Proactively scouting for causes to fund and support

→ Do you want to **receive proposals**? If so, do you have the **capacity to manage** that process?
→ Do you want to **scout for causes and partners**? If so, do you have the capacity to **explore the field thoroughly**?
→ Would a **blended** or ad **hoc approach** suit you?

NOTES

Relationships

RESTRICTED ———┼─┼─┼─┼──┼─┼─┼─┼─── **UNRESTRICTED**

Giving to an organization for one specific project only

Once you have selected the organization(s) you want to support, you can decide to fund specific activities or projects. We call this restricted or earmarked giving in which you will be able to jointly monitor expectations and possible changes in transparency and focus. Your partners will also value the predictability of your funding. On the other hand, you can decide to make grants to an organization without a specific project or activity in mind. In philanthropy, we call this unrestricted giving. This offers flexibility to the partner organization, but it can be more challenging to receive a detailed, transparent narrative about your contribution. Your partners might appreciate having room for maneuvering in how to use the financial resources.

Giving to an organization with flexibility and not limited to a specific project

→ Do you prefer to be **highly targeted** in your giving, in terms of **specific projects**?
→ Would it make more sense to **give more generally** and allow your partners to **use funds** as they **see fit**?
→ Would it be helpful to **blend** the **two approaches** in some way?

✏️ **NOTES**

_____

_____

_____

_____

UNILATERAL ———|——|——|——|——|——|——|——|——|——|——— COLLABORATIVE

Giving solely

"If you want to go quickly, go alone. If you want to go far, go together." In philanthropy, you can work on your own or in multiple combinations with others. Given that a foundation does not have shareholders, "clients" or an owner, a foundation enjoys a unique freedom to act. Decide whether you would prefer the quick decision making and autonomy of flying solo, or whether you would prefer to include other donors or foundations in your philanthropic journey. Collaboration can lead to new ideas, new networks and this can lead to better results, but it also requires greater coordination.

Giving in collaboration with others

→ Do you want to go it **alone** in your giving? If not, how **collaborative** do you want to be with others such as **foundations** or **other partners**?
→ How much **freedom** do you want in your giving?
→ How does this **relate** to the **focus** and **ambitions** of your philanthropy?

Insight

LOOKING FOR INDEPENDENT BOARD MEMBERS

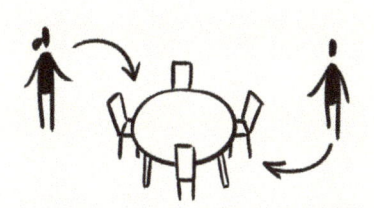

"In our family business, deciding to have non-family members sitting on our board was a key success factor. In our foundation, we can manage this among ourselves."

We often hear this from philanthropic families we work with. Family philanthropy can often be about assigning productive roles and responsibility for family members. When a foundation has dedicated non-family staff members, this might be the right approach. But, even so, we believe that including non-family members on the board, organizing board retreats with external facilitators and conducting external evaluations of your giving are healthy ways to make sure you do good and are good at doing it.

Partners 109

Relationships

Good Practice in Building Strong Relationships with Partners

Giving is not a science, but an art. However, some general best practice principles can give a frame to your style of giving and build healthy relationships with partners:

Head and Heart
As you build your relationships and develop your structures for giving, you will also come across special one-offs and areas that touch you ("heart") but that might not be in your initial strategy ("head"). We encourage you to ringfence about 15% to 20% of your resources as a reserve for giving to special interests, or those driven by your heart. Philanthropy, while usually very organized, should remain a tool to facilitate your generosity – be it in a structured way or simply responding to a call for compassion in one-off cases.

Select Partners First
Your grant making is about making a difference. Individuals in leadership positions and their team are the ones that make it happen. We recommend that your choice of partner organization should be driven by a careful assessment based on your criteria. You can then, in confidence, jointly define the projects you will support to realize your goals.

Be a Reliable and Consistent Donor
Long-term commitment – from three to five years minimum – is recommended if you seek lasting change and impact through your giving. We also recommend that you are explicit about your funding cycle and the likely exit of your support. This helps your partners plan and budget effectively.

Light Touch Engagement
Strict frameworks and structures are helpful to understand mutual expectations. However, you also need to have a light touch to allow your partners to fully devote their attention and resources towards the beneficiaries.

Be Both Ambitious and Humble
Humanity is faced with major challenges and philanthropy can make a big difference. But, sometimes, change is hard to measure. It can be helpful to compare your experiences and expectations with other donors or independent voices.

Insight

EQUAL PARTNERS

In the past, philanthropy was framed as a one-way relationship between donors and recipients. The complexity of the challenges that the world faces, and the aspirations of donors to be more involved in a more professionalized world of philanthropy, is leading to a new era of giving in which donors and recipients choose to join forces and act together. This more collaborative approach is seen by both parties as a mutual journey of close partnership that offers benefits for all. Fewer donors see themselves as knowing all the answers or wanting to impose solutions. In fact, effective philanthropy treats its entire ecosystem as a community of equal partners, working together with one collective aim. The donor drives the philanthropy activity but is heavily influenced by a close and supportive ecosystem. Within that, the recipient of the resources, whether a small or large charity or a fishing fleet in a developing country, plays an equally vital role in achieving the aims of the project.

Relationships

Activities

With your exploration of the importance of partners in philanthropy now complete, you can move towards defining what kind of partners will best support your giving and how to include them in your giving. The following exercises will help you make these important choices. For new philanthropists, this means selecting your initial tribe of external partners. For existing philanthropists, it is an opportunity to reflect on your current network and to make any changes that might be necessary.

Family Philanthropy Navigator Questions:

→ Who do we need or want to partner with, outside the family, in order to implement our giving?

Activity 1:
Review Your Trade-Offs

Step 1

Review the trade-offs in this chapter and, individually, answer the following questions. Use different colors to visually highlight the two questions in each of the trade-offs. You can position yourself anywhere along the spectrum from one end to the other end of the trade-off.

1. **Where is our philanthropy today?**
2. **Where would I like our philanthropy to be in the future?**

Step 2

As a family, compare and discuss where each one of you marked dots for "where are we today" and "where would we like to be". What are the similarities and differences? Where are you aligned or not? How can this further shape your journey?

Step 3

If there are any differences in your perspectives, discuss how you wish to address these.

* Note to aspiring philanthropists:
If you are not yet philanthropically active you can simply focus on question 2 in Step 1.

Partners

Relationships

**Activity 2:
Partners as Advisors**

Once you have reflected on the trade-offs and options available within the ecosystem of partners, it is time to focus on formulating the "non-family" partners that will complete your team. The following activities will guide you through this process.

NAME OF THE PARTNER

Contribution
How could they support you in your philanthropic endeavor?

Step 1

Complete Your Tribe
Review the table you filled in for Activity 2 in the previous chapter on **Family Involvement** and identify how you might seek additional support and benefits from working with selected outside partners, such as co-donors, advisors, board members, etc. Are there any gaps in terms of knowledge, expertise, network access or other types of resources that you think should be filled by outsiders?

Step 2

Map Out Your Wider Ecosystem for Impact

You now have a clearer understanding of your crew, composed of family members as well as selected outside partners. However, this might not be enough to fulfill your mission. You might want to consider spinning a web that goes beyond your "inner circle" and form a dense ecosystem of partners, ambassadors or key opinion leaders, who may also be able to help you achieve your goals. Along the lines of the below illustration, you may wish to identify core categories of support partners and then identify key players to include in your journey.

Partners

Relationships

**Activity 3:
From Family Values to Criteria and Selecting Partners**

Values drive and shape your giving. They help you to understand the context in which you give and what you want to achieve individually and as a family. This exercise will help you reflect on your core personal values, and to find common ground with members of your family.

This process can be useful to agree a set of fixed values that can serve as the moral compass for your family, to identify values that you wish to pass on to the next generation or to refine existing values. This will also help you to understand your values can be instrumental in selecting the kind of organization(s) you would like to support and work with.

If you and your family already have defined your values, then you can jump directly to Step 5, unless you wish to co-create new, shared values.

Step 1

Each family member should go through the illustrated list of values and select their top five values as well as their five "maybe" values that could be considered as a backup in case of any misalignment. Feel free to add any additional values if they are not represented in the table.

MY TOP 5 VALUES

1. _____
2. _____
3. _____
4. _____
5. _____

MY 'MAYBE' 5 VALUES

1. _____
2. _____
3. _____
4. _____
5. _____

LIST OF VALUES

Fun Inner peace Social responsibility
Curiosity Generosity Gratitude Love Optimism
Diversity Discipline Loyalty Kindness Equality
Adaptability Duty Motivation Unity
Integrity Altruism Openness Passion
Empathy Faith Success Honesty Recognition
Health
Authenticity Harmony Humility
Fairness Creativity Reliability Frugality
Caring Achievement
Cohesion Independence
Compassion Autonomy
Competence Humor Legacy Reputation
Performance Responsibility
Impact Courage
Spirituality Peacefulness
Forgiveness Environment Learning
Leadership
Respect Friendship Relationships Happiness
Wisdom
Engagement Innovation Tradition Confidence
Service Empowerment Stewardship Trust Vision

Relationships

Step 2

Share your top five values with your family and aggregate your top values on a single sheet.

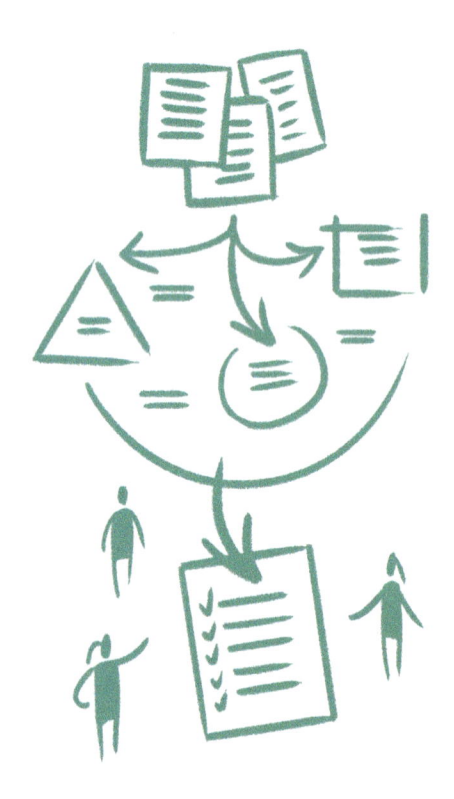

Step 4

Use a voting system to agree on your family's top five values, with a possible list of "maybe" values as a backup.

Step 3

Cluster your collective family values by theme or category.

OUR TOP 5 VALUES

1. _____
2. _____
3. _____
4. _____
5. _____

OUR 'MAYBE' 5 VALUES

1. _____
2. _____
3. _____
4. _____
5. _____

Step 5

Giving is about making choices. Therefore, it is helpful to define criteria for the decisions you will have to take regarding whom to support and whom not to support. In this step, we ask you to explain how each family value can be translated into your criteria for selecting partners.

Step 6

As a subsidiary question in building a clear relationship policy with your beneficiaries, we recommend that you address the following questions before making any initial grants:

→ What is the ideal duration of the support you plan to make? (years)
→ How formal would you like your support to be? (e.g. e-mail or contract)
→ Would you like to have a direct relationship with the partners you support or work solely through intermediaries?
→ Will you plan a formal exit policy as part of your giving?

VALUE	MEANING FOR SELECTING PHILANTHROPIC PARTNERS
e.g. Performance	*It is important that a partner can show us how they perform and what results they have achieved from the funded activity. The criteria could, for instance, be: 1) impact or 2) efficiency in using resources.*
1.	
2.	
3.	
4.	
5.	

Partners

Relationships

Case Study
The Bloom Fund

In Conversation with Sara Ojjeh and Lia Ojjeh Martin

> "It's important to respect differences within the family and in each other's journey."

- **Name:** The Ojjeh family

- **Country of origin:** Switzerland

- **Family size (total number of family members):** 10 family members (including spouses)

- **Background information about your family's legacy and current business activities:** Our family has a longstanding history as investors in multiple areas, including motorsport, medical technologies, sustainable agriculture and aviation.

- **Which generation are you part of?** 3rd generation

- **Number of family members involved in your philanthropic activities:** Four siblings and spouses. Parents with hands-off involvement.

Areas of giving

Focus of Giving
We focus our impact in health and education. More recently, we also started giving to refugee-related causes.

Country/Region
We give or have given in mainly three continents: Europe, Africa and Asia.

Other Aspects Worth Noting
Our family has developed an ability to transform its giving over generations. The first generation's giving was driven by a religious duty and the third generation's giving is driven by family values.

Structure of giving

Type of Structure
We give through two main channels:

1. Bloom Fund - Philanthropic giving overseen by four siblings and spouses. Family members equally contribute their financial resources to the fund. The fund is managed by external philanthropic advisors.
2. Ethos Philanthropies Consulting - Philanthropic consulting firm founded by three sisters.

Our family philanthropy has never been linked to business giving or corporate social responsibility.

Family Governance/Decision-Making
All of our family members (including spouses) are equal partners in decision-making. There are no formal policies or documents to regulate our giving. The approach is that family comes first, and our decision-making is very value-driven.

OJJEH FAMILY

GIVES THROUGH 2 MAIN CHANNELS

BLOOM FUND
• OVERSEEN BY 4 SIBLINGS + SPOUSES

ETHOS PHILANTHROPIES CONSULTING
• CONSULTANCY FIRM RUN BY 3 SISTERS

NO FORMAL POLICIES OR DOCUMENTS TO REGULATE THE GIVING

FAMILY COMES FIRST!

FAMILY MEMBERS ARE EQUAL PARTNERS IN DECISION-MAKING

VERY VALUE-DRIVEN

Case Studies

Relationships

Navigator Questions

Family involvement

→ **Who from our family is/will be involved? What is the nature of that involvement?**
We, as four siblings, and our spouses dedicate our funds and time to the Bloom Fund. Additionally, the three sisters are very engaged in running their philanthropy consultancy firm. We are equal financial partners.
We jointly make the important decisions about all our philanthropic projects. Everybody plays, depending on their capacity at that given time, more of an active role or more of a supportive role. We have this adaptability and fluid approach in our roles based on what we are going through in our lives. Everybody is able, at different times, to take the reins, to step forward, to be the front person.

As a family, we made a long-term financial commitment and we also made a strong emotional commitment to our beneficiaries. We, as four siblings, our spouses, and our parents, are really the ones that are involved in philanthropy – everybody is involved in different capacities and in a way that is flexible.

Partners

→ **Who do we partner with/need to partner with, outside the family, in order to implement our giving?**
We partner with external philanthropic advisors to research and help implement our projects. We also appoint a specific project leader to each project. The main vehicle of giving, the Bloom Fund, is named as an acronym of the siblings' and their spouses names. This model allows the family to focus solely on giving and delegate the administrative burden.

KEY LEARNINGS AND RECOMMENDATIONS

1. **Family comes first.** It's important to respect differences within the family and in each other's journeys. Originally, it had started out as a democratic process when it came down to our giving: from deciding on certain funding structures to sums and grants. But if two of us were for it and the other two against it, how would we navigate that? Because our main value is that family comes first, we worked to build a system of active listening and agreeable terms to navigate potential disaccord.

2. **Fail forward.** You only fail if you fail to learn from your mistakes. Grants might fail. Projects or processes will fail. We had a couple of grants that did fail; money that was unable to be traced or inability to measure the impact. Sometimes you don't reach the goals that you hoped to achieve; sometimes the change isn't as sustainable as you hoped it would be. Embrace your mistakes as a learning opportunity so that you become better at what you do over time.

3. **Inspire, don't dictate.** Don't try to dictate what younger generations should do and be open to innovation and evolution. The idea is to share what you've learned and to give them enough room to take from it what is going to help them grow in their own right. When working with your family members (especially the younger generation) or other philanthropists and partners share to inspire, not to dictate

4. **Develop your own philanthropic identity.** There are multiple different ways of being a philanthropist. There are all sorts of different ways that you can develop yourself as a philanthropist without going through traditional structures. You don't have to give big, international grants that need to be managed from afar. You can, but you don't have to. There's a huge upcoming generation of people who are going to be philanthropists in their twenties and thirties and forties; it's not an "afterlife" thought. They're building their philanthropic profile at the same time as their career profiles. You too can create your own space to share ideas, partner and give together.

5. **Get involved.** Be hands-on, ask questions and visit projects you support – all key learning happens in the field. Create new meaningful conversations with your family. Involvement with partners teaches you humility when considering the size of the challenge.

6. **Partner with others.** As active and younger philanthropists, we have realized that a lot of times wealth can be isolating. Having the possibility to learn from each other, partner and give together is paramount. Finding the help and partners you need to become an effective philanthropist can be hard.
"You cannot be the money in the bank, and the boots on the ground, and the program manager; you cannot do it all alone."

7. **Don't hide.** Don't hide behind anything. Tell your story if you want to. It's not about ego; it's about experience and learning. Initially, we were very private about our philanthropic activities – all giving was done anonymously. But, today, as a modern, adult philanthropists, it is amazing to be able to share about our successes and failures, and to use our name to tell the story hoping that there maybe are other philanthropists who can identify with what we have done in philanthropy and leapfrog from our learnings.

Case Studies

Relationships

Case Study
The Oak Foundation
In Conversation with Kristian Parker

"Place trust in your staff. Place trust in your partners."

→ **Name:** Kristian Parker, the Oak Foundation

→ **Country of origin:** Switzerland

→ **Family size (total number of family members):** 15

→ **Background information about your family's legacy and current business activities:**
The resources of the Oak Foundation originated in the Duty Free Shoppers business which my father, Alan Parker, helped to build. The 1st and 2nd generation have worked together to create program areas within a family foundation.

→ **Which generation are you part of?**
2nd generation

→ **Number of family members involved in your philanthropic activities:**
Six family members (two from 1st generation, three from the 2nd generation and one from the 3rd generation)

Areas of giving

Focus of Giving
The Oak Foundation, established in 1983, runs seven programs focused on policy advocacy – environmental issues (oceans, Climate and wildlife), human rights, preventing child abuse, issues affecting women, housing and homelessness, learning differences, and special interests.

Country/Region
Global, with special programs in Denmark, Brazil, India and Zimbabwe.

Other Aspects Worth Noting
We established a professionally run foundation to manage programs that are developed by family members, based on their own interests. The foundation is limited in terms of size - we can hire a maximum of 100 staff.

Structure of giving

Type of Structure
Family foundation, grant making.

Family Governance/Decision-Making
Our decision-making is strategic.
The family regularly asks questions like:
Have we done everything we can?
Have we successfully achieved our goals?
What are have we learned?

Case Studies 125

Relationships

Navigator Questions

Family involvement

→ **Who from our family is/will be involved? What is the nature of that involvement?**
My parents, when they set up the foundation, had an expectation or a hope that it would remain a family foundation, which means that it should be controlled by the family and run by the family. Therefore, the family is closely involved in our foundation. Each family member spends a different amount of time with the projects they are involved with. We all take part in activities such as hiring staff, defining strategy, approving grants, site visits, overseeing finances as well as administrative aspects of the project.

The board is comprised solely of family members as final decision makers. Prospective family board members who want to join the board need to be at least 25 years old. For future family board members who have not reached the age of 25, we get them involved in grant making before they become board members. They can also attend board meetings occasionally, to get a feel for what the board does. They can take more and more responsibility, if they wish, over time. For now, we have six board members with the potential for 12.

Partners

→ **Who do we partner with/need to partner with, outside the family, in order to implement our giving?**
We invite non-voting advisors such as a lawyer, a doctor who, amongst other things, teaches ethics, and someone with a background in civil society and philanthropy to join our board meetings to challenge and advise us. We employ a non-family president, professional staff, program directors, program officers, and assistants.

We work extensively with a wide network of partners in order to implement our giving strategy. We rely on our partners to deliver our goals so we invest in existing institutions and NGOs with core funding, listen to them to help build their strategy, and trust them to deliver the right solutions. We co-invest in our partners with other foundations, because we believe that a beneficiary should not become overly dependent on one source of funding. Therefore, we tend to provide no more than 50% of an organization's budget (ideally, we aim at 20-30%). We believe that co-funding is an effective strategy to prevent dependencies and to leverage each other's resources. We also actively create new organizations to facilitate and encourage collaborations (e.g. Oceans 5, European Climate Foundation, Partners for a New Economy), as well as to share and learn with other donors (e.g. Climate Funders Table).

KEY LEARNINGS AND RECOMMENDATIONS

1. **Support good governance.** The good governance of your partners is key. They need to have strong boards, balanced out by a strong executive. The COVID-19 crisis, for example, was a time when you would have discovered weaknesses in your partners, and it was a moment for reflection for everyone. Therefore, we extended core funding to some of our key partners so that they could build reserves and survive the crisis. Because they deliver something that no one else can deliver easily without creating an organization, which is extremely difficult and expensive, we decided to be flexible and extended our financial support. To have an impact, you will need strong partners with great leadership and a solid governing body. To achieve that you will need to invest with core funding in your partners, but it will pay off over the long term.

2. **Be inclusive.** Build inclusion into your giving model to capture the diverse interests of your family. As a family with varying interests, we have developed a model that strikes a balance between individual freedom for family members to develop their own programs with dedicated staff alongside light oversight from the group of trustees. At a very specific level, we can each individually approve a grant of half a million (USD) without other family members getting involved.

3. **Delegate when appropriate.** Hear the voice of your partners and delegate when appropriate. To gain greater impact, you will also need to delegate decision power to your partners. Acknowledging our limitations, we tend to create new platforms to facilitate giving outside of our foundation. This helps our partners to build their own capacity and take responsibility, along with some decision-making power.

4. **Trust and learn.** Place trust in your staff. Place trust in your partners. Learn from your partners. You probably don't know better than the field. Every couple of years, we run a grantee survey to learn how we are doing relative to the past in terms of support and responsiveness.

5. **Mind the power dynamic.** You won't achieve impact on complicated issues without working with others – and that requires compromise. If you've decided that you have the best strategy on the planet and you've worked it out to every last detail before you talk to anybody else, it's not going to work very well. If you don't listen to the field, the dynamic of the money relationship will sabotage your success because they will tell you what you want to hear.

Relationships

Case Study
The Carvajal Foundation

In Conversation with Manuel Jose Carvajal

> *"A company cannot prosper indefinitely in a sick social environment; because sooner or later society's problems will affect its performance."*

→ **Name:** Manuel Jose Carvajal, Chairman of the Board of the Carvajal Foundation; member of the Council of the Foundation

→ **Country of origin:** Colombia

→ **Family size (total number of family members):** 230 members of the family, excluding in-laws (about 300 including in-laws). Note: in-laws are not treated as family for governance purposes.

→ **Background information about your family's legacy and current business activities:** Our family founded Carvajal S.A. in 1904 in Cali, Colombia, focusing on a variety of business fields including packaging, office and school stationery, trade, textbook and phonebook publishing, today our main lines of business are packaging, paper manufacturing, IT Services and school stationery; we employ around 19,000 employees in 14 countries in the Americas.

→ **Which generation are you part of?** 4th generation

→ **Number of family members involved in your philanthropic activities:** 18

Areas of giving

Focus of Giving
Our foundation focuses on three themes:

1. Income generation: teaching microentrepreneurs how to run a business; and teaching employability skills to individuals with low incomes to improve their employability.
2. Education: improving the quality of basic education and early childhood care.
3. Community development: training leaders in the community to be more effective in their roles.

Country/Region
Cali and Buenaventura in Colombia.

Other Aspects Worth Noting
We created our family foundation in 1961 with the goal of improving the well-being of disadvantaged people in the local community, based on the idea that you cannot have a healthy business in a sick social environment. According to its bylaws, the foundation's giving cannot benefit the company in terms of corporate social responsibility.

To support all descendants of the original owners, in the late 1990, we created a social dividend. The idea behind it is to provide subsidies in three areas: education, health insurance, and housing to all family members whether or not they are engaged with the business.

Structure of giving

Type of Structure
The Carvajal Foundation is an operating foundation. It owns 22.3% of family company's shares (as of 2020). Its annual budget is, on average, USD 10 million (NB: budget numbers are pre-COVID). Through our foundation, we employ 52 full-time team members and up to 700 part-time staff for various projects.

Family Governance/Decision-Making
The funding for our foundation consists of:

→ 25% is from dividends of the shares it owns in the company;
→ 75% from donations or grants from entities which include other businesses, Colombian or international NGO, and local, regional and national government.

Our foundation has a Foundation Council that plays a supervisory role and its members meet three times a year. The Foundation Board is involved in the day-to-day running of the foundation.

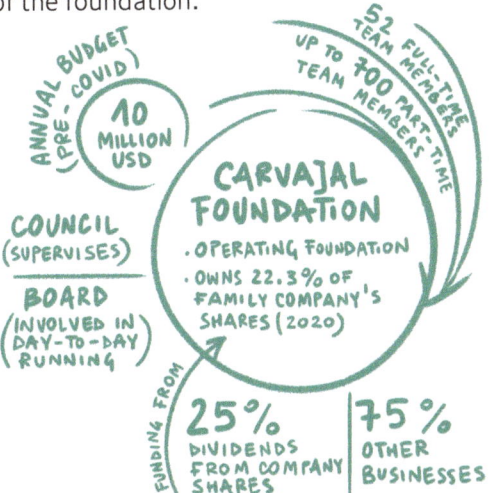

Case Studies

Relationships

Navigator Questions

Family involvement

→ **Who from our family is/will be involved? What is the nature of that involvement?**
The Foundation Council is composed only of family members, and the Board is composed of six family members and three non-family members. The foundation's CEO reports to the foundation's board.

Family members have worked in the foundation in different capacities throughout its history. The type of work varies according to their interests and experience. We have had family members who worked as CEO, in communications or finance. For our younger generation, we offer a summer internship program to learn about the company and other entities the family has, including the foundation and our philanthropic activities.

Employment in the foundation is open to all family members as long as there is a need and the person is qualified. In the recruitment process, if we have a family member and a non-family member who are equally qualified, we prefer to hire the family member, but otherwise we pick the more qualified candidate.

Partners

→ **Who do we partner with/need to partner with, outside the family, in order to implement our giving?**
We partner with international NGOs and businesses as well as local, regional and national governmental agencies, and work in alliances to increase the scope and reach of our giving. By "partners" we mean individuals or organizations who offer either funds or know-how. The number of alliances or partnerships we have is very large. Therefore, we "build bridges" between the different players in our community. We operate in an ecosystem and, to achieve systemic impact, we support a multi-stakeholder approach.

KEY LEARNINGS AND RECOMMENDATIONS

1. **Institutionalize your giving.** We sent a clear, strong message to the family and our community that we were making a permanent commitment to our philanthropic endeavors by creating a separate entity to carry out the family's mandate and gave it a purpose, its own bylaws, an endowment, a governance structure, and staff. It's also stated in the bylaws that if, for some reason, the foundation is liquidated, the shares that it owns have to be given to an entity that does similar work - it cannot go back to the descendants of the original donors.

2. **Reflect on and transform your giving.** Be transparent in assessing how effective your programs have been in the past, explore with great curiosity the needs of your partners and beneficiaries, visualize the "ideal future," and transform your giving accordingly.

3. **Build bridges.** Some of the biggest challenges in the world are too big for one entity to resolve alone. Mobilize your entire ecosystem to achieve the impact you wish to see. There is no "them" and "us." Together, we can achieve more.

4. **Prepare for your exit.** Plan for your exit early on and empower your partners in order to prevent any dependencies. Your planned and well-executed exit can help your partners thrive as they continue their journey.

5. **Aim for systemic impact.** We have worked in entrepreneurship for many, many years, but we still have a very high unemployment rate in our region. Therefore, we started asking: With the work that we have done, how much have we impacted unemployment? How can we learn to work in new ways that will allow us to have a greater effect?
Therefore, we decided to do things differently. We promoted the creation of a collective that include the Secretary of Education, the teacher's union, representatives of local universities, and other foundations and civic groups to do a diagnostic of the education system and develop a vision for it for the next 15-20 years. This group started working together – and it's amazing how we all moved forward to achieve this impact.

6. **Allow for synergies with CSR.** Historically, we have had a wall between the company's CSR and the foundation. In the foundation, many years back, we started working with recycling. In our region, recycling is the lowest of the lowest priorities. But, at the same time, one of our biggest businesses is in packaging and it produces a lot of plastic cups and plates. To address the problem of plastic in the company, we decided to leapfrog on the know-how that the foundation has developed over the years. That is one way in which we are starting to connect the dots between our philanthropic efforts and the business. You may also want to rethink how to create synergies between your company's CSR and your philanthropy.

Case Studies

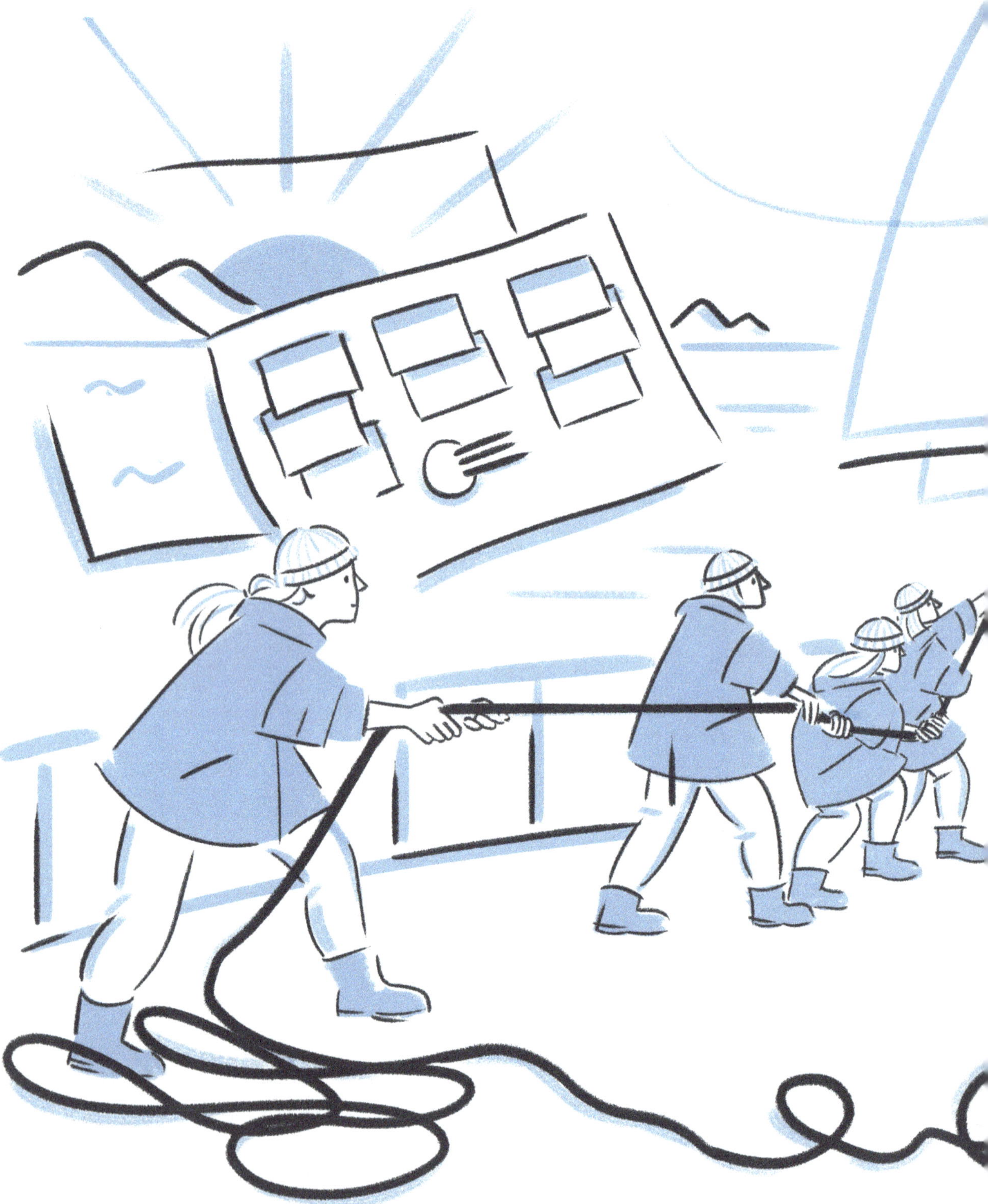

Organization

138 **Resources**

148 **Governance**

170 **Impact**

186 **Case Studies**

Organization

Introduction

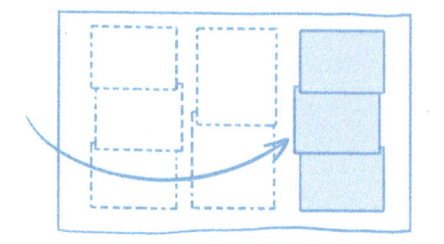

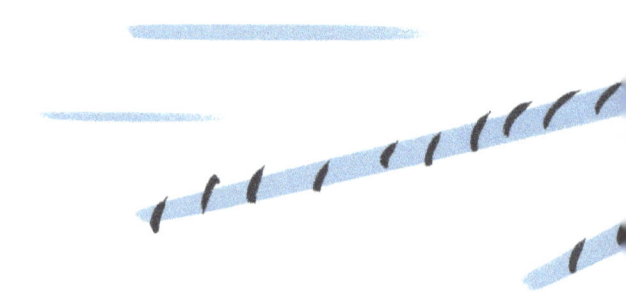

What resources would you like to give?

Are you giving money only or also offering your own time and energy? How will you structure your giving? Will you set up a foundation or donate individually to personal projects? Who will make the big decisions, and how? What oversight and governance mechanism will you put in place? How will you assess and improve the impact of your giving?

At this stage in your journey through the *Family Philanthropy Navigator*, you will have considered and made some crucial choices about the purpose of your giving and the relationships that will power your giving. You have developed a clear understanding of your motivation, focus and ambitions, as well as the role you, your family and other partners will play.

From this point on, your philanthropic journey turns from concept into reality. It's the moment for you to think about how you wish to organize your giving. You will need to define what resources are required and available to you and how you plan on managing and deploying them in the most effective and efficient way to achieve your goals. You will also need to select the governance, structures and decision-making processes that you think will serve your purpose best. Finally, you should think about how you measure and monitor the impact of your giving.

The main navigator questions that you and your family will answer at this stage are:

> → **Resources**: What do we give? What do we need? How do we fill the gaps?
>
> → **Governance**: How do we structure our giving? What rules, processes and policies help us?
>
> → **Impact**: What is the desired impact of our giving? How do we know that we have achieved it?

This might seem overwhelming and somewhat technical at first. However, this is an essential step in your philanthropic journey, and it is incredibly important that you devote the necessary time to each of the above questions. Finding the right organizational setup and structure will ultimately decide whether your philanthropic journey is as successful as you want it to be.

The way you structure your giving may also lead you to reflect on and reshape some of the choices you made earlier in the book. For example, by reflecting on the resources you have and need to achieve your goals, you might reconsider who from the family you wish to involve (and how) and what number and type of non-family partners you wish to engage in the process.

It's clearly a journey-defining fork in the road and requires careful reflection and discussion before settling on any solution. While there is no right or wrong organizational model for giving, take time to assess the various options available to you before you move ahead and turn your thoughts into action. You can shape and refine your philanthropy at any moment, but once you have put in place an organizational structure it becomes more complex and time-consuming to change direction.

Introduction 135

Organization

This is a unique opportunity to consider how you wish to embed your family's giving into the wider family enterprise system. As outlined in the Purpose section of the book, many enterprising families leverage philanthropy as a mechanism to share values and knowledge across generations, foster inter-generational collaboration, onboard and educate the next generation or involve otherwise less-engaged family members. If one or more of these motivations apply to you and your family, you will need to carefully contemplate the resources you have and the additional resources you need, as well as the type of governance model that will enable you to achieve these family-related goals.

Resources

What resources do you need to achieve your aims in giving? Where will those resources come from? How will they be managed? This chapter will help you determine what resources you can and want to give, and what resources you would need to source from your partners. While there exists a wide range of conceptual frameworks that describe different types of resources, we suggest differentiating between four categories: treasure, time, talent and ties.

Insight

REMEMBER YOUR PURPOSE

Throughout your philanthropic journey, do not lose sight of your purpose and be prepared to revisit and reflect on it at different stages. The nature of your purpose is key to designing the organizational structure of your giving. Whether you are motivated to support a cause you deeply care about, aim at bringing your family closer together, or hope for some positive spillover effect for your business, it is advisable that you remember the reasons that drive you to give as you progress through this part of the navigator.

Governance

What type of structure will suit your circumstances and goals? What roles will family and non-family members play in this structure? How will decisions be taken? Choosing the right setup and governance for your giving is the most important step towards making things happen. Structuring your giving will help you manage your resources effectively and ensure that your giving is sustainable, whether in the short-term or across generations. It will also solidify how strategic decisions are made, as well as what oversight and management rules and processes are in place. While there are many differences in regulations between countries, this step will provide insights on the most common ways of structuring philanthropic activities.

Impact

Ultimately, philanthropy is about impact. How do you achieve impact relative to your purpose? How do you choose to measure and monitor that impact? How can you optimize your impact over time? You may have grand ambitions but does the impact of your philanthropy meet those goals? While your intentions may be noble and your organization might be watertight, it is important to remember that the impact of any philanthropic activity could turn out to be positive or negative, and that there is a difference between achieving results and having an impact. In this chapter, we will explore ways to help you deliver your desired impact as a philanthropist.

Organization

Resources

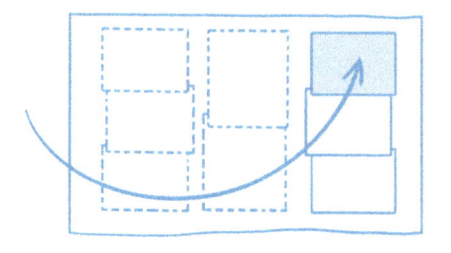

Setting the Scene

Philanthropists support specific causes by providing various forms of resources. While the most common type of resource given by philanthropists is money, giving is not just about money.

In the broadest sense, we can differentiate between four main types of resources that philanthropists can give, which is summarized in the widely used "4T" framework: treasure, time, talent and ties. For example, you could support a regional museum by donating money, or you could donate or lend your art collection to this museum, or you could donate your time by becoming an ambassador of the museum, or you could leverage your network to promote it.

Depending on the purpose of your giving, as well as how you are planning to involve family members and partners, the types and amounts of resources you are likely to provide may differ. The way you balance these four elements will vary from case to case and depend on your and your family's interests, skills, availabilities and financial assets. While it could be that you only provide one type of resource, a philanthropic journey often entails a myriad of resources and activities. For example, donating money, evaluating organizations that you support, attending grant-maker gatherings, visiting projects "on site," sharing results from your projects, giving feedback, raising awareness about your cause, sharing a philanthropic experience with your family, learning about the best practice in the field, mobilizing your network of friends to support the cause you are passionate about, or building and maintaining relationships with partners.

As the field of philanthropy professionalizes and expectations for transparency, accountability and impact grow, we believe that families might benefit from a more rigorous and well-structured approach towards mobilizing and deploying resources to the causes they wish to support. We argue that in the increasingly complex and interdependent world we live in, it is difficult to be truly effective in giving without taking a thoughtful approach to ensure the careful allocation of your resources within an appropriate, well-governed organization.

Many causes and needs around the world are highly complex and deep-rooted, and it is very unlikely that one philanthropist will have all the resources necessary at their disposal to cure them. As you draw on and allocate resources, it is important to align your giving with a realistic appreciation of what can be achieved, in line with your purpose and partners' expectations.

Based on our research and experience, "best practice" philanthropists adopt a pragmatic and rigorous approach to allocating and orchestrating their resources. That is, they tend to run their philanthropic organizations as efficiently and effectively as possible, with clear structures, roles and responsibilities, and goals.

The total resources and engagement that you, your family and wider network can dedicate to your philanthropy will also help you determine what setup and governance will work best for your giving. Mobilizing resources in a harmonized and holistic way will help you to achieve your desired outcomes.

Organization

Setting the Compass

In the following pages, we will describe and explore trade-offs that will inform your thinking and help you and your family structure meaningful discussions about the resource allocation for your philanthropy.

As outlined earlier, there are many ways to give and there is no one right answer. However, you will need to come to an agreement in terms of who will give what and how much in order to bring your philanthropic journey to life. Take some time to reflect carefully as an individual and family on each of the following areas.

Insight

CREATE A FINANCIAL SAFETY NET

It is important that you and your family discuss and agree on the types and amounts of resources that you can give. We would also advise that you create a financial safety net to ensure the continuity of your philanthropic projects. For example, if your donations are derived as a percentage of your business profits, you might want to put a mechanism in place to ensure philanthropic commitments are met, especially if you engage over numerous years alongside organizations you have selected. This is important so that beneficiaries can rely on your support even in times of adversity. You could also consider acquiring additional resources from your support network and external partners, although this implies a greater responsibility in reporting back on the progress made and might involve additional work for you.

FINANCIAL RESOURCES ONLY ├─┼─┼─┼─┼─┼─┼─┼─┤ **INCLUDING NON-FINANCIAL RESOURCES**

Giving financial assets only

A crucial decision that you and your family will need to make is whether you will only give financial resources (as grants, donations, co-funding) or whether you will also get more personally involved by giving other types of resources such as your time, talent and ties. This relates to the "hands-on" or "hands-off" question, and how collaborative you want to be in your giving. Giving time, talent and ties implies that you will be more involved in the process to some extent, while giving money suggests that you will rely more heavily on partners.

Giving other resources such as time, talents and ties, as well as finance

→ What **type** of resources do you want to give?
→ What **balance** of resources is **appropriate** for your circumstances?
→ How much **time** in a week or a month do you **wish to dedicate** to your philanthropic activities?
→ What **skills** and **experience** can you and your family bring to the table?
→ What **networks** and **ties** can you tap into?

NOTES

_____
_____
_____
_____

Organization

FAMILY MONEY ONLY |——+——+——+——+——+——+——+——| **INCLUDING NON-FAMILY MONEY**

Giving from family financial resources exclusively

The way you fund your philanthropic activities, and whether you prefer to keep it in the family or are open to raising money from other donors, is a fundamental question. The latter approach adds a layer of responsibility and accountability where non-family donors may expect to be informed about or even involved in the governance of your philanthropy. Giving only family resources can give you a lot of control over these resources. It can also be a positive way to engage passive family members or to empower the next generation. However, it usually requires greater family involvement and greater responsibility to your beneficiaries.

Additionally leveraging others' financial resources or fundraising

→ How much money do you **plan to commit** to philanthropy?
→ Will you **fund** your giving from **family finances** or **external sources**, or both?
→ What level of **startup** and **ongoing administration** costs are you comfortable with?

NOTES

Family Philanthropy Navigator

PERPETUAL —|—|—|—|—|—|—|—|—|— **DRAW DOWN**

Funding your giving from interest earned from an endowment, dividends, or a percentage of business profits

Some families organize their giving in a perpetual way, while others give in a strictly time-limited fashion. A perpetual model could align with an expectation that future generations of your family will remain engaged with your giving, while the draw down model can be deployed to respond to pressing needs in the world and might fit with family preferences to engage in a limited way.

Dedicating a certain amount of resources to a specific cause that is spent in its entirety

→ Are you and your family in it for the **long haul**?
→ Do you wish to **build** a philanthropic organization that will give in a **perpetual way**, using family funds over a long period time?
→ Are you looking to spend down **certain funds** or deliver **funding over generations** through interest from **endowments**?
→ Do you want to fund projects and causes with **set funds** over a **limited timeline**?
→ Do you want to respond to **one-off needs** only?

NOTES

Organization

Activities

You have now completed your consideration and exploration of the important topic of resources. Taking time to make careful and pragmatic choices for the requirements, sourcing and allocation of resources in line with your purpose and relationships is a crucial part of any effective approach to giving. The following activities will help you and your family clarify and then answer the critical navigator questions for resources as they relate to your circumstances and as you begin or refine your journey in philanthropy.

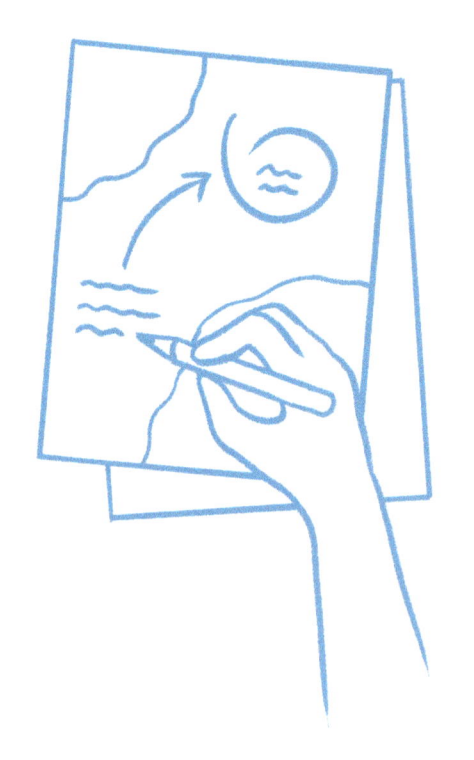

Family Philanthropy Navigator Questions:

→ What do we give?
→ What do we need?
→ How do we fill the gaps?

Activity 1:
Review Your Trade-Offs

Step 1

Review the trade-offs presented earlier in this chapter and, individually, answer the following questions. Use different colors to visually highlight the two questions in each of the trade-offs. You can position yourself anywhere along the spectrum from one end to the other end of the trade-off.

1. **Where is our philanthropy today?**
2. **Where would I like our philanthropy to be in the future?**

Step 2

As a family, compare and discuss where each one of you marked dots for "where are we today" and "where would we like to be". What are the similarities and differences? Where are you aligned or not? How can this further shape your journey?

Step 3

If there are any differences in your perspectives, discuss how you wish to address these.

* Note to aspiring philanthropists:
If you are not yet philanthropically active you can simply focus on question 2 in Step 1.

Resources 145

Organization

**Activity 2:
Resources Matrix**

Having decided in previous chapters on your giving ecosystem of family and partners and the nature of their involvement, this matrix will help you to map out how to access all the resources that you think are critical to successfully launch or grow your philanthropic organization.

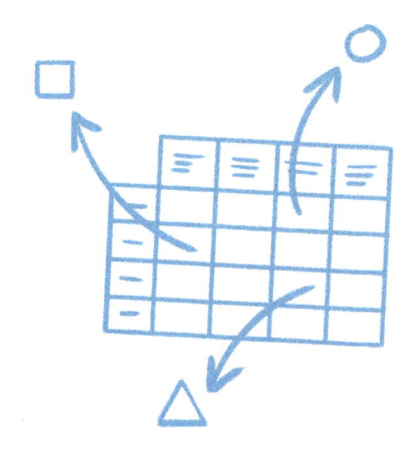

Step 1

Resources Needed
The first important step is to identify the type and amount of resources needed in order to achieve your philanthropic ambitions. For this step we suggest that you take a "blank sheet" approach without considering any resource constraints. What is truly needed to be successful?

Step 2

What Resources Will I Give?
Each family member should map the resources that they can bring to the table. We suggest that you first do this exercise individually, considering what you could contribute before engaging in a detailed discussion as a family.

Step 3

Map Your Family's Overall Resource Contributions
Share your contributions and draw the overarching picture of resources that are provided by the family.

Step 4:

Identify Gaps
As a next step, we recommend you compare your needs (Step 1) with your family's overall contributions (Step 3) to identify possible gaps you might have.

Step 5

Leveraging Partners to Fill the Resource Gaps

Finally, you conclude with a clear idea of where all necessary resources will come from and what the next steps are to access, harness and roll out those resources.

For already active philanthropists, this exercise will provide a valuable opportunity to take stock of how resources are managed and where improvements or changes can be made.

What will I give?	**What will my family give?**	**How much can I and my family give now?**	**What else do we need from non-family partners to realize our philanthropic initiative?**

Treasure

Time

Talent

Ties

Organization

Governance

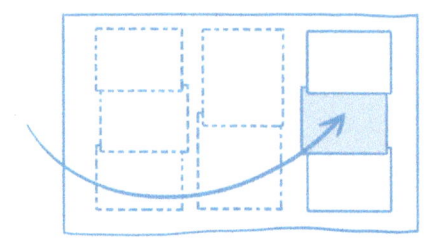

Setting the Scene

Having worked through the previous chapters of the *Family Philanthropy Navigator*, you should now have a clear idea of what you want to do as a philanthropist and why, who from your family and outside your family will be involved and how, and what resources are available to you within your ecosystem of giving.

The next step is to use this information to decide on the best way to set up, run and govern your philanthropic activities. While, as in many aspects of your journey, there is no right or wrong approach, there will be certain governance models that are better suited to what you wish to achieve.

You should weigh your options carefully before moving forward, taking into consideration the conclusions from your navigator journey so far and seeking advice from peers and experts in the field. Establishing inappropriate or unclear structures and governance could result in less than desirable results and create unwanted tensions within the family.

Contrary to popular belief, running a philanthropic organization doesn't differ that much from running any other type of organization, even if the legal framework conditions are different. If you aim to build and maintain a healthy and effective philanthropic organization, it will require principles of good governance on multiple levels. It is vital in ensuring that your activities are efficient, effective and well-managed.

148 Family Philanthropy Navigator

DEFINITION

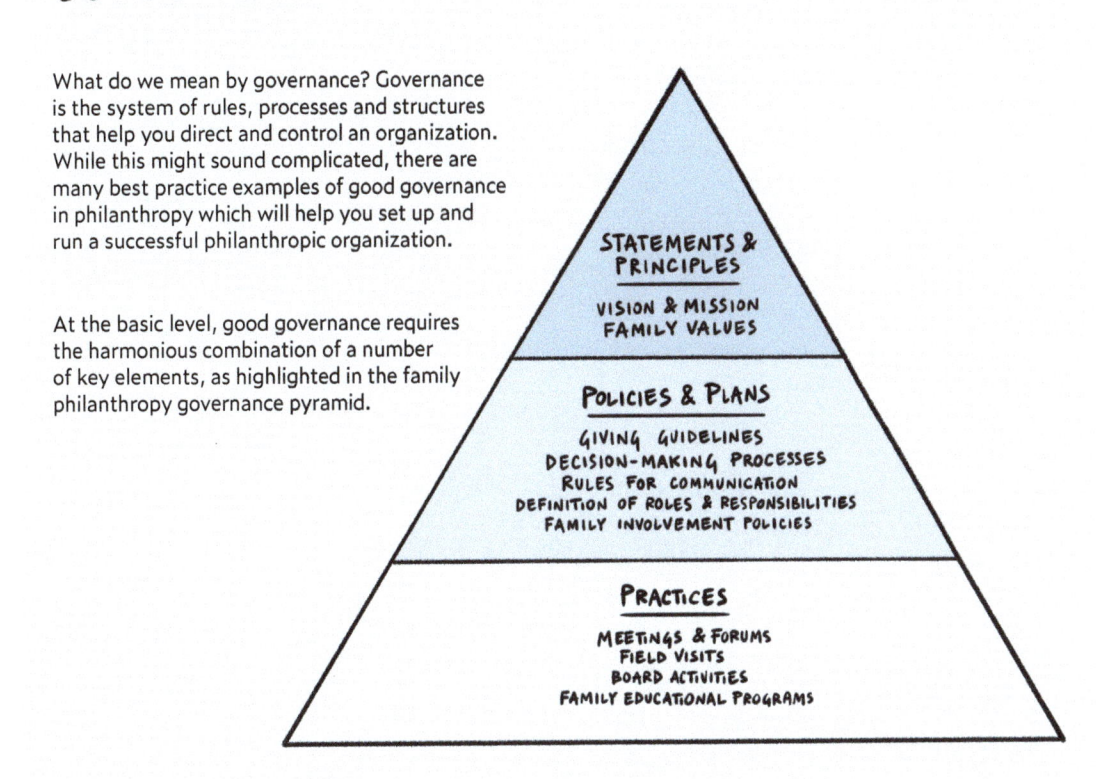

What do we mean by governance? Governance is the system of rules, processes and structures that help you direct and control an organization. While this might sound complicated, there are many best practice examples of good governance in philanthropy which will help you set up and run a successful philanthropic organization.

At the basic level, good governance requires the harmonious combination of a number of key elements, as highlighted in the family philanthropy governance pyramid.

STATEMENTS & PRINCIPLES
VISION & MISSION
FAMILY VALUES

POLICIES & PLANS
GIVING GUIDELINES
DECISION-MAKING PROCESSES
RULES FOR COMMUNICATION
DEFINITION OF ROLES & RESPONSIBILITIES
FAMILY INVOLVEMENT POLICIES

PRACTICES
MEETINGS & FORUMS
FIELD VISITS
BOARD ACTIVITIES
FAMILY EDUCATIONAL PROGRAMS

Organization

Deciding On the Appropriate Structure for Your Giving

The structure you choose is a means to an end. However, it is an important step because it formalizes many of the reflections you have had so far. In addition, some of the choices you make in terms of structure can be quite difficult to change over time because grants are irrevocable. While philanthropy is often related to the structure of a foundation, there are numerous options available that may also depend on the fiscal context of the country in which you are a resident.

There are many tried and tested philanthropic structures that you could adopt for your giving, from one-off donations or ad hoc grant making to a charitable trust or independent foundation. Although we cannot present an exhaustive list of structures from different contexts and countries here, we have selected what we believe are the generic setups worthy for your consideration:

Direct donation: a gift made directly to a public charity.

Endowment: a donation of money or asset to a public charity to provide on-going support to that organization.

Donor advised fund (DAF): a charitable giving vehicle administered by a public charity created to manage donations on behalf of organizations, corporate families, or individuals.

Public interest foundation: an independent grant making structure that is usually funded by regular gifts or a specific endowment from a single source such as an individual, a group of individuals or a corporation. It is important to stress that the foundation has no owners and no shareholders.

Charitable trust: a three-party fiduciary relationship in which the first party, the settlor, transfers assets (often but not necessarily a sum of money) to the second party (the trustee) for the benefit of the third party – the beneficiary (in our case, a charity).

Choosing from the options above depends on a number of factors such as the intention of the founder(s), the resources you have (the 4 T's), the visibility you want to give to your philanthropy, or even the duration of your intended project.

Two important factors include how much money you are planning to give and how much you and your family wish to be involved. For example, if you are directly donating money to a museum to construct a new building or to a university to create a Chair, the governance to oversee and manage that approach is going to be relatively straight forward. At the other end of the spectrum, if you decide to support a project or organization working with autistic children or on fighting climate change, you will be engaging in a lengthier endeavor and you will need to build knowledge and develop a network of partners. In other words, in the initial illustration, this might be a one-off gift while in the latter you engage in an entrepreneurial journey that will involve more commitment. Hopefully, it is clear that you don't need the same structure in both cases.

The following illustration might help you make the appropriate choice for your structure. We strongly believe that the structure you choose should be based on a reflection of your resources, as defined earlier. If you make a one-off grant, then you are likely to be in the left and lower side of our diagram below. If you have more financial resources and more time to spend on an issue then you will move to a more complex, but also to some extent, more rigid structure, moving right and upwards in the diagram.

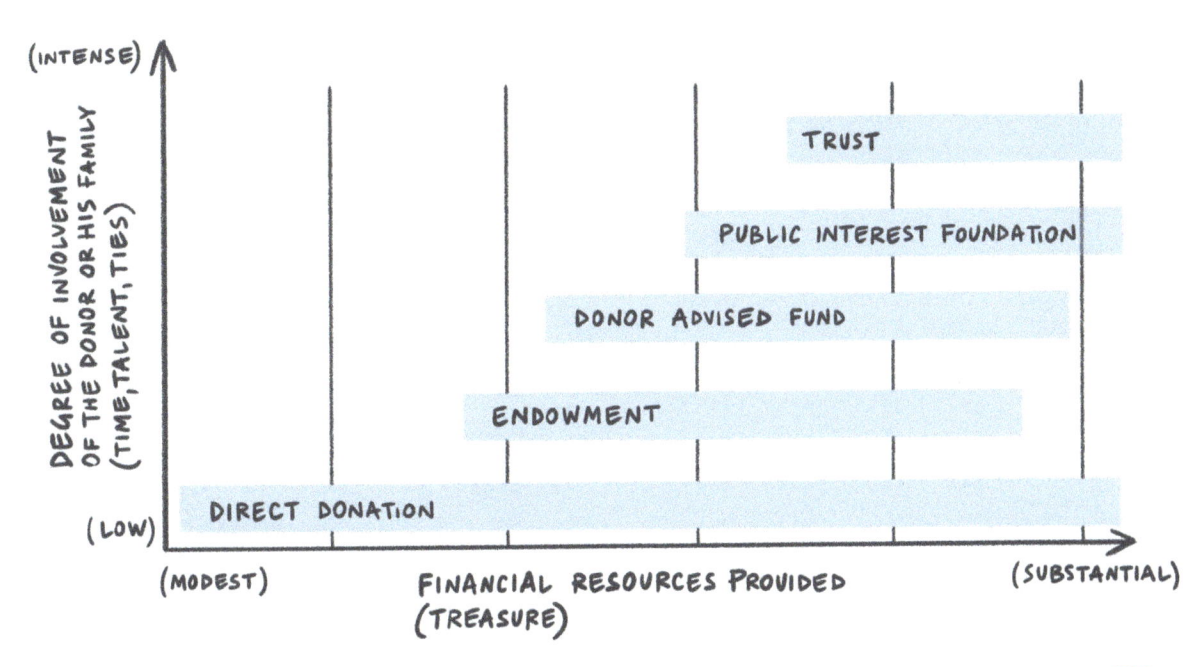

Governance

Organization

While those options lay down the main routes, the following concepts are also worth considering:

→ **NextGen funds:** Some family foundations (usually public interest foundations) create a compartment within the main foundation that is dedicated to the grant making of the next generation. This can be deployed to facilitate the distinct focus of their giving, and to educate them about the governance of a foundation and joint decision making.

→ **Donor collaborative funds:** Over the years, issues like marine biodiversity or artificial intelligence in warfare have reached such a level of complexity that donors and foundations have decided to regroup part of their grant making into an umbrella structure to leverage each other's resources. This often takes the form of a DAF. It can include individual donors but also family or corporate foundations. In the case study of the Oak Foundation, Kristian Parker refers to some similar endeavors that the foundation is involved in.

→ **Corporate, family and independent foundations:** These all refer to the same legal entity of a public interest foundation. However, depending on the founder or founding entity, they will be labeled differently. Relationships will need to be clarified for each. For example, who will sit on the foundation board or from where will financial resources come from.

→ **Shareholder foundations:** These are foundations that own a (part of a) company and, at the same time, also have a public interest purpose. In that sense, they have both an economic and social mission. They are a variation of the public interest foundation.

Insight

ADJUST THE STRUCTURE OF YOUR GIVING TO YOUR SITUATION

It is advisable that you consider and plan ahead for how your philanthropy may evolve over time because things are in constant flux. On the one side, as you evolve from nascent and growth stages to maturity, you gain more experience and you may feel the need to iterate or fine-tune the setup and governance of your giving. On the other side, families and ownership groups evolve across generations, requiring different types of governance mechanisms in order to handle the wishes and needs of a different (and often larger) group of stakeholders.

Embed Your Philanthropy into the Wider Family Enterprise System

As we've seen before, there are a number of different structures you can choose for your philanthropy. The ultimate choice of structure and governance is also dependent on a number of factors that pertain to your specific family enterprise system, which illustrates the full range of activities that enterprising families are involved with and how they are interconnected.

Is there an overarching purpose that connects what we do in business and what we do in philanthropy? How does philanthropy fit into the wider range of activities of the family, ownership group or business? What are some of the strategic connections between our family's various activities? Do we want to leverage our family office as a structure or resource for our philanthropic giving? Does our philanthropic work align with or complement our other investment activities? What role does the family council play in our philanthropic work? Do we wish to leverage philanthropy in order to educate and onboard the next generation?

These are just some of many questions you and your family ought to ask when it comes to embedding your philanthropy within the wider range of your activities. It is worth considering how you could make your philanthropy cohesive and aligned with existing governance structures, protocols and values within your family, ownership group, business or family office.

This holistic view is particularly useful for the purposes of the *Family Philanthropy Navigator* as it allows families to unlock synergies and efficiencies, ensure long-term continuity while also providing reassurance to the family. If you are already involved in philanthropy, this is an opportunity to reassess your current structures for giving to ensure it is fit for purpose and also right for your family; in particular, the current or next generation.

When integrating your philanthropic giving within the family enterprise system, there exist many options to connect the dots and find alignment.

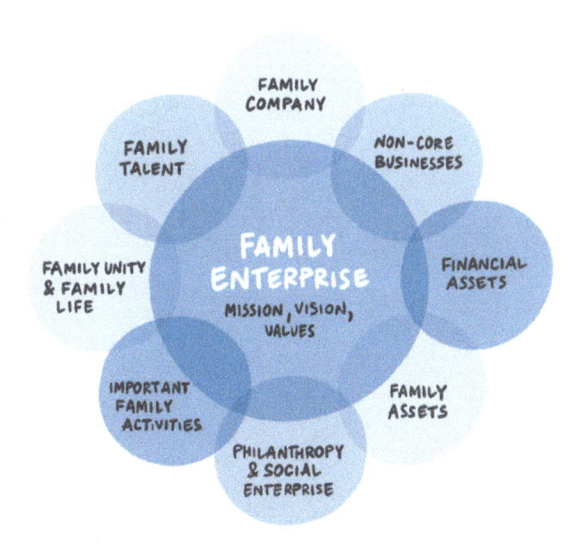

John A. Davis, Cambridge Institute for Family Enterprise, 2013

Organization

The following graphic extends on the well-established three-circle model, illustrating the family, business and ownership group and the main governance mechanisms that you could consider leveraging for your philanthropic activities, including the family office.

Clearly, all family enterprise systems are unique, and you might not necessarily have all of these governance mechanisms in place, which is not a problem. You also wouldn't necessarily leverage all of them at once. Instead, the graphic intends to provide an overview of different possible interconnections within your wider governance model.

Here are a number of questions you might wish to consider when it comes to deciding which governance mechanisms to leverage and connect with your giving:

→ What is the size and complexity of the family and ownership group?
→ Do you wish to involve the entire family or ownership group or just part of it?
→ How established is your existing governance in the family, ownership and business? Would it make sense to formally leverage the governance mechanisms for your philanthropy?
→ Do you have an established family office that you could leverage for part of the activities related to your philanthropy? If yes, which ones?

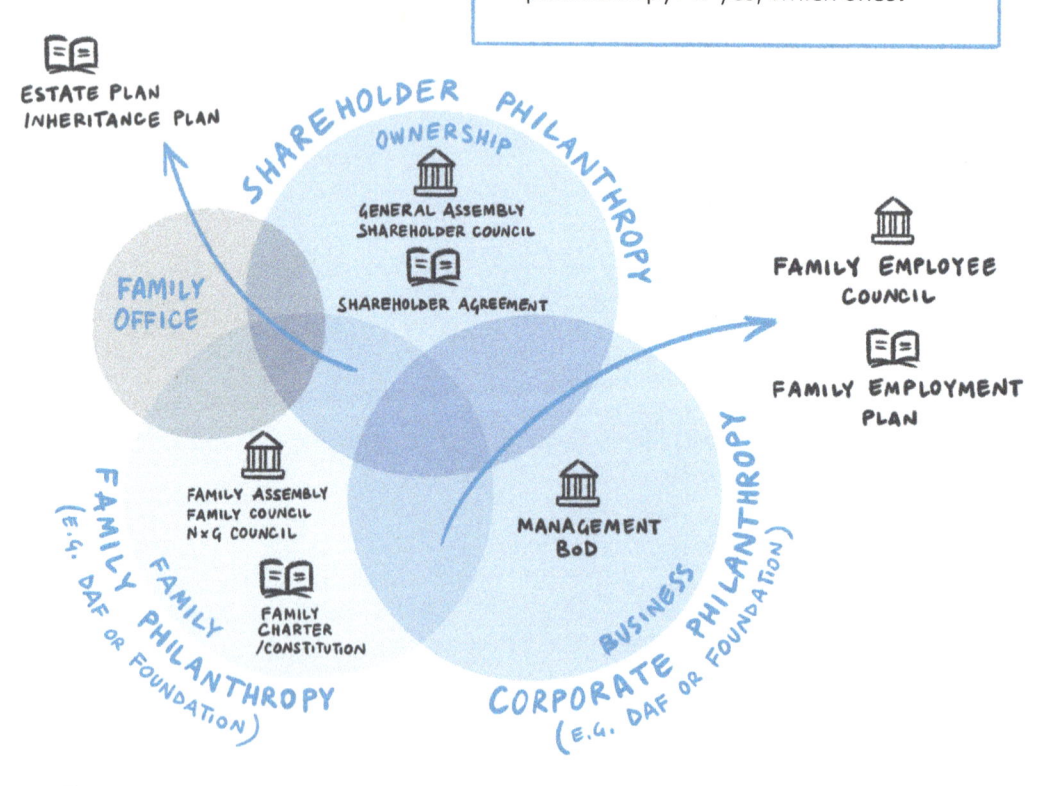

ESTATE PLAN
INHERITANCE PLAN

SHAREHOLDER PHILANTHROPY

OWNERSHIP
GENERAL ASSEMBLY
SHAREHOLDER COUNCIL

SHAREHOLDER AGREEMENT

FAMILY OFFICE

FAMILY EMPLOYEE COUNCIL

FAMILY EMPLOYMENT PLAN

FAMILY ASSEMBLY
FAMILY COUNCIL
NxG COUNCIL

MANAGEMENT
BoD

FAMILY CHARTER
/CONSTITUTION

FAMILY PHILANTHROPY
(E.G. DAF OR FOUNDATION)

BUSINESS PHILANTHROPY

CORPORATE PHILANTHROPY
(E.G. DAF OR FOUNDATION)

154   Family Philanthropy Navigator

Existing family and ownership governance systems play a critical role in the philanthropic journey of many families. Larger families often establish a philanthropy committee or working group – either within their family council or also including members of the wider family. The next generation council is also frequently included, given that philanthropy can be leveraged to onboard and educate the next generation, as outlined in the Motivation chapter earlier in the book. These are, therefore, excellent starting points to formalize and anchor your philanthropy.

Some of the core principles, values and desired outcomes of philanthropy are often in the family charter (or constitution). As this is not a legally binding document, but a moral agreement between family members to ensure alignment, it is not uncommon to include a section on philanthropy. The family charter can also include a section on family employment, which might not only relate to the business(es) but also to philanthropy, especially if you establish a more formal structure such as a foundation. Who, under what preconditions and qualifications, is entitled to be on the board or work for the foundation? This is another important question to consider for larger and more complex families.

When it comes to the more technical matter of resource allocation in philanthropy, families occasionally leverage the shareholder agreement to formally agree on the amount allocated for giving. This is particularly helpful if you wish to ensure continuity of philanthropic support across generations, during times of economic downturns or when decision making in the family might be difficult. Some families also decide to endow their philanthropic foundations from their family trust as in the case of the Ishk Tolaram Foundation.

The family office is frequently involved in a family's philanthropic activities. You might have a foundation as a vehicle for giving with family members sitting on its board and leverage your family office for various administrative and organizational aspects such as collecting and screening incoming requests, setting up meetings, organizing field visits, among other things.

In the case of corporate philanthropy, you may wish to link it with your existing business governance and leverage specific board members or executives from the business to support you in your philanthropic efforts, either by sitting on the board of the foundation alongside the family or by organizing a separate philanthropy committee which acts as a bridge between the family, the business and the corporate foundation. The cases of the Mauvernay family as well as the Fark Holding nicely illustrate such governance approaches.

Another great example of multistakeholder interaction and collaboration within the family enterprise system is the Ahlström Collective Impact (ACI), which was introduced by the Eva Ahlström Foundation (see case study in the Purpose section) in 2020, as a model for collaboration between the foundation and the partnering companies.

Organization

Insight

DEALING WITH CONFLICT IN FAMILY PHILANTHROPY

Many aspiring philanthropists have the expectation that philanthropy will become a positive shared experience for their family. While well-managed, collaborative philanthropy can be beneficial for family relationships, existing tensions between family members cannot be healed through a shared philanthropic experience. In fact, family issues may escalate as members make important decisions about the legacy of their ancestors or the distribution of their wealth.

Here are five common sources of conflict in family philanthropy:

1. **Cause.** Should we keep supporting a cause that the family has historically supported but we no longer have a strong emotional connection with, or should we support causes that we care about today?

2. **Geography.** Should we keep supporting the city, region or country where our founder came from, even if we no longer have a relationship with that place?

3. **Role.** Can a specific family member have an important role in the business and philanthropy, or might this trigger some conflict of interest or unfair treatment vis-à-vis other family members?

4. **Rivalry.** Do we have branch representation or merit-based representation in our philanthropic giving?

5. **Multigenerational tensions.** Is the senior generation holding on to decision making and control or can the next generation take responsibility?

There are many ways to set up a family's philanthropic activities and connect or integrate them with their wider family enterprise system. While there is no one-size-fits-all approach, there are different best practice examples to learn from. It is vital that you and your family take a conscious decision on what might be the best governance structure for you and which types of pre-existing governance mechanisms to leverage. This will ultimately also relate to the question of decision making, which we will explore next.

Decision Making

How are grant-making decisions made? How formal or informal should the decision-making process be? Which governing bodies take which decisions? No matter what type of setup you select, decision making will form an important part of your giving. When designing your decision-making processes, there are important factors such as family dynamics, family size, family structure as well as existing ways of taking family decisions that you need to consider.

The majority of families follow the decision-making procedures that are established in their foundation bylaws – typically requiring a majority vote or unanimity. It is important that you and your family think about and agree on the most appropriate decision-making process before you actually venture out and start your philanthropic journey. This also depends on the ultimate structure you choose and how you connect your giving with the other governance bodies within the family enterprise system.

Insight

PICKING A NAME

Picking an organization's name must be done with great care. Families are often keen to honor their founders or engage the next generation by naming their philanthropic organization after certain relatives. There are certain advantages and disadvantages to a family's reputation and business if they are too closely linked with a family's philanthropic organization. Do you want to cherish the legacy of one specific family member (e.g. grandmother or grandfather) or is it about more than just one individual? Here are some options to consider:

1. Name the foundation after one specific individual (e.g. Eva Ahlström Foundation).
2. Name the foundation after the family (e.g. Carvajal Foundation).
3. Name the foundation with a link to the business (e.g. Tolaram Foundation).
4. Name the foundation with abbreviations of family members (e.g. Fondation Juniclair or Bloom Fund).
5. Create a symbolic or family-unrelated name (e.g. Oak Foundations, Fondation Philanthropique NEXT).

If you don't clearly spell out how decisions will be made, you might end up in a conflicting situation that leads to tensions within the family that could have easily been avoided if the rules of the game had been defined upfront. We recommend that you and your family first reflect on the full range of decision-making options, select the most appropriate option for your family and only then start the process of actually taking decisions.

However, as with every decision that is taken inside a family, these can be incredibly time-consuming and frustrating processes. Even if you have an explicit approach towards decision making, other family dynamics can kick in and bypass the formal governance you have created. A typical challenge arises when one board member (e.g. the founder or parent) has more influence than others and, as a consequence, their opinion implicitly carries more weight than that of the others. This can be particularly frustrating for the next generation, for outside advisors or board members who have been hired to help professionalize giving. It is therefore important that all family members understand and, as much as possible, follow the governance the family has agreed on.

As in business, different decisions might require different decision-making approaches. Here are three common approaches:

Governance   157

Organization

Unilateral decision-making

- → This approach is a quick and efficient mechanism that is useful for trivial or uncontroversial decisions or decisions that need to be made in a very short time (e.g. disaster or emergency grant making).
- → We also often find this type of decision making in the early phase of a philanthropic engagement, before formal governance structures are in place.
- → Within enterprising families, we are often confronted with unilateral decision making (e.g. because there is one dominant family member).

Board voting with majority

- → This approach is a decision-making mechanism that might be required by the bylaws for a certain type of decision and is a process that involves all board members. It leads to a definite outcome based on whether a majority is reached or not.
- → Board voting with majority can also be a useful mechanism when philanthropy spans across and involves different parts of the family enterprise system, such as the family, the business, the ownership group, the family office, etc.
- → Voting is often considered as a fallback option in case consensus cannot be reached.

Consensus-based decision-making

- → Consensus-based decision making may be required by the bylaws for very important decisions (e.g. discontinuing the foundation) and is a mechanism that typically involves a lot of discussions that ultimately lead to consensus; thus, resulting in shared understanding and buy-in.
- → Consensus-based decision making can also be the sign of a very healthy and well-functioning family, ownership group or business board. We know from best practice, corporate boards that decide based on consensus quite naturally only in rare instances have to resort to majority voting.
- → However, when there are different views, which is inevitable in a family or family enterprise system, this can become a very time-consuming process. Any attempt to reach consensus might trigger other forms of conflict (depending on the family dynamics). As such, it might not be the most appropriate form of decision making for every family and every decision.

It is of critical importance that you clearly spell out who, or which governing body, will take what types of decisions and based on what types of decision-making mechanism. Aligning this with your overall governance will help you establish a more effective and efficient philanthropy.

Effective Boards for Giving

Boards are vital in many family philanthropic journeys for decision making, oversight, as well as to empower and involve family members and other partners. To ensure your board is fit for purpose, it is important that you ask yourself a number of important questions related to board composition, board structure and board policies.

Board Composition
- Do you include the immediate family only, or also the extended family? Can in-laws get a seat on the board? What happens in case of a divorce? Do you award your children with seats on the board? What is the minimum and maximum age limit to join the board?
- Do you want non-family and independent professionals to join the board? If so, what would be their role and the level of their participation? If not, how would you source subject area expertise to support the family only board?
- What are the responsibilities of each board member? How will board members be sanctioned or removed if they fail to meet these responsibilities?
- How does your board relate to your mission and strategic priorities? What challenges would the current composition of your board entail?

Board Structure
- How many board members do you wish to include? How many family members can join?
- How often does the board meet?
- Do we want to establish committees (e.g. finance committee) within the board or not?

Board Policies
- How is board membership shared among siblings and family branches? What are your criteria for selecting family and non-family board members? Are there any prerequisites in terms of skills, capabilities and expertise in order for family members to be considered for a board role?
- What policies do you need to put in place to bring clarity to the board, now and in the future?
- What are the term limits and rotations?
- What tools can the board use to streamline the planning process?
- How can the board and staff communicate effectively?
- What is your conflict resolution policy?

Organization

Setting the Compass

In this section, we will describe trade-offs that we have encountered during our research and experience of working with enterprising families. We suggest that you take some time to explore these areas to guide and inform your and your family's decision making while setting up your philanthropic organization and designing your governance structure.

NOTES

FORMAL ←——————————→ **INFORMAL**

Setting up formal procedures and rules within your giving organization

You will need to make a number of decisions related to how formal or informal you want your giving to be. Your approach may vary over time between operating in a very formal way within your philanthropic organization or giving in a more informal way without setting up procedures or rigid rules. Perhaps the most important decision to make is whether or not to set up your own philanthropic structure or to give directly to specific organizations or causes that take the organizational side of things out of your hands.

Giving in a more ad hoc and informal way, without formal procedures or rules

→ How **structured** and **formal** do you want your giving to be?
→ Will you only give to **already existing** organizations?
→ Would you prefer to establish **own giving** organization(s)?
→ Will you set up a **board** or not?
→ Will you employ **staff**?
→ How will you approach **financial** matters such as **tax** optimization?

Family Philanthropy Navigator

Insight

TAXES

Although tax exemption is never a sole reason to engage in philanthropy, it is important to consider what benefits and costs of giving apply to your context. Before choosing your giving setup, inform yourself about the rights and responsibilities that each specific setup will entail. Be prepared to be challenged by philanthropy skeptics about the motivation of your giving.

PUBLIC PROFILE ⟵――――――――⟶ **PRIVATE PROFILE**

Building a public image to support your goals in giving

Some philanthropists develop a public profile deliberately, while others favor a discreet approach. There can be compelling family and business reasons for both. If advocacy is a key part of your philanthropic journey, then there are clear advantages that derive from being in the public eye. It can help in attracting partners and additional donors. However, you might want to operate below the radar to let your partners do their work away from the spotlight. This approach can make sense if you have security concerns, for example.

Deliberately staying out of the public eye

→ Will a **public profile** support your philanthropic goals?
→ Would a **lower profile** be more appropriate?
→ What **family** and **business factors** might influence this decision?

NOTES

_____
_____
_____

Governance

Organization

LINKED TO THE FAMILY ├┼┼┼┼┼┼┼┼┤ **LINKED TO THE BUSINESS**

Giving that is primarily linked to your family and family governance

Some families link their giving to family interests, values and governance structures. Others prefer to align their philanthropy with their business activities. In a developed family enterprise system, it might be more appropriate to give in a way that fits into the whole, cohesive ecosystem. In practical terms, you could link your giving directly to your business or give through a separate private entity. Keep in mind that, depending on your motivation, the choices here might differ. If your motivation is to unite the family and educate the next generation, you might be better off selecting an independent vehicle. However, if you seek to do good in an area that is strategically aligned with the purpose of your business, you would likely establish a corporate foundation.

Giving that is primarily linked to your business and business governance

→ Do you prefer to align your giving to your **family values** and **governance**?
→ Would an **independent structure** be more appropriate for you?
→ Is your giving **related** to your business's **focus areas**?
→ Would it make sense to create a **corporate foundation**?
→ Is your family enterprise system **highly cohesive** or **less integrated**?

NOTES

FAMILY LED ├──┼──┼──┼──┼──┼──┼──┤ **LED BY NON-FAMILY**

Family board members only, family executives, vehicle size limited to what is appropriate for the family

Leading any type of formal family philanthropic organization requires substantial family involvement. While there are many roles that family members can play, including at board level, as advisors or hands-on managers, many families account for the fact that family involvement cannot be taken for granted by choosing a setup where non-family staff can fill in critical gaps. Depending on the purpose of your giving, the degree of family involvement and the resources being deployed, you can assess whether it would be best that your philanthropy is family-led or not.

Managed by non-family members reporting to a board that ideally consists of both family and non-family members

→ To what extent will your structure be **governed** and **led** by family members?
→ What are the **limitations** and **expectations** for your family?
→ Will you need to **tap external resources** to implement your giving?

NOTES

_____
_____
_____
_____

Governance

Organization

Activities

Having read through the various options with respect to the governance of your philanthropic giving, it is now time to make some choices. As compared with some earlier chapters, this chapter might require some more deliberate reflection (individually and as a family) and consultation of outside expertise (e.g. regarding legal and tax implications in certain countries) in order to arrive at a definite answer. However, we still wish to help you initiate this reflection process.

Family Philanthropy Navigator Questions:

→ How do we structure our giving?
→ What rules, processes and policies help us?

Activity 1:
Review Your Trade-Offs

Step 1

Review the trade-offs in this chapter and, individually, answer the following questions. Use different colors to visually highlight the two questions in each of the trade-offs. You can position yourself anywhere along the spectrum from one end to the other end of the trade-off.

1. **Where is our philanthropy today?**
2. **Where would I like our philanthropy to be in the future?**

Step 3

If there are any differences in your perspectives, discuss how you wish to address these.

* Note to aspiring philanthropists:
If you are not yet philanthropically active you can simply focus on question 2 in Step 1.

Step 2

As a family, compare and discuss where each one of you marked dots for "where are we today" and "where would we like to be". What are the similarities and differences? Where are you aligned or not? How can this further shape your journey?

Organization

> **Activity 2:**
> **Aligning On Some Key**
> **Governance Parameters**

Step 1

Map Out the Status Quo
As a first step, we recommend you and your family map out your current family enterprise system and list its various governance mechanisms (for the family, the ownership group, the business), leveraging the frameworks introduced earlier in this chapter (pages 153 and 154).

Step 2

Identify Possibly Links with Your Philanthropic Activity
Once you have mapped out your family enterprise system and listed all the existing governance mechanisms, you can start thinking about possible links and connections with your philanthropic activity. Do any of your existing governance mechanisms (e.g. the family constitution) already have a link to philanthropy that you can build on? Are there any gaps in your current governance with respect to philanthropy that should be filled in order to advance your cause?

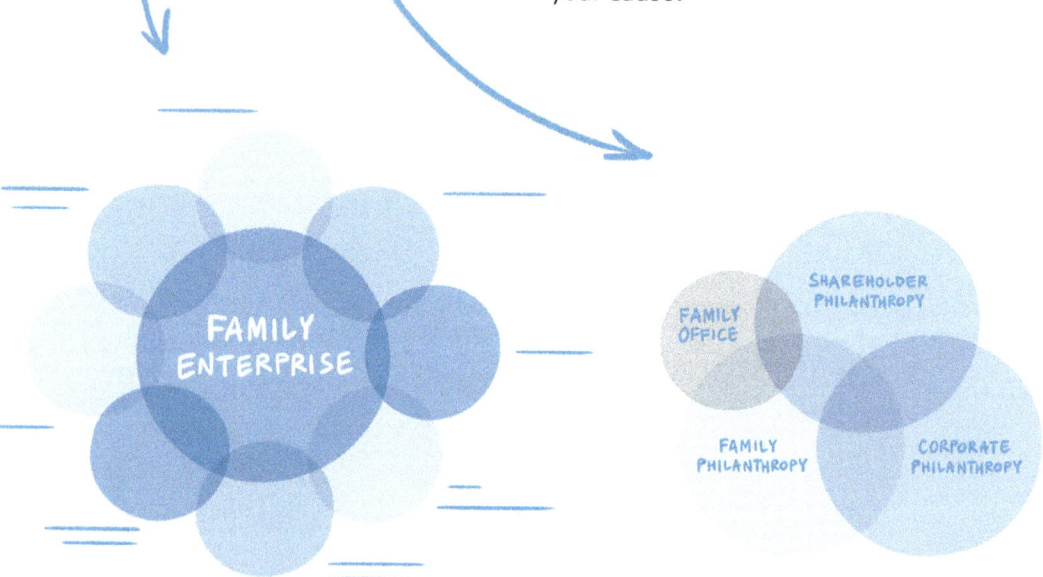

FAMILY ENTERPRISE

FAMILY OFFICE · SHAREHOLDER PHILANTHROPY · FAMILY PHILANTHROPY · CORPORATE PHILANTHROPY

Step 3

Define Your Preferred Structures

Going through the various options for how to structure your giving, as outlined earlier in this chapter, think about what the most suitable structure for your giving might be. You will not necessarily arrive at a final decision on this without some outside advice, but start thinking about whether you have a preference, as a family, and what might make most sense. Depending on whether you want to focus on family philanthropy, shareholder philanthropy or corporate philanthropy (or a combination of all three), you can then think about the various governance mechanisms – in the family, ownership group, and business – you will need for your philanthropic activity, and any possible adjustments you might need to make (e.g. do we need to include a section on philanthropy in our family constitution or shareholder agreement?).

Step 4

Map Out Initial Thoughts On Decision Making

As a last step, think about how you would like to take decisions.

→ Which decisions would we like to take as a family, and which governing body should be taking them (e.g. family council, philanthropy committee)?
→ How will we be taking decisions as a family (e.g. on projects, financial matters, strategic matters)?
→ Which decisions do we delegate to other governance bodies within our family enterprise system (e.g. family office, company board of directors)?

Organization

**Activity 3:
Aligning On Some Key
Governance Parameters**

Step 1

To help you think about the best governance approach to take, work out how to structure your giving by completing the following table.

Which decisions would we like to take as a family, and which governing body should be taking them (e.g. family council, philanthropy committee, next generation council, family office)?

How will we be taking decisions as a family (on projects, financial matters, strategic matters, etc.)?

Which decisions do we delegate to other governance bodies within our family enterprise system (e.g. family office, company board of directors)?

How formal do we want our philanthropy governance to be?

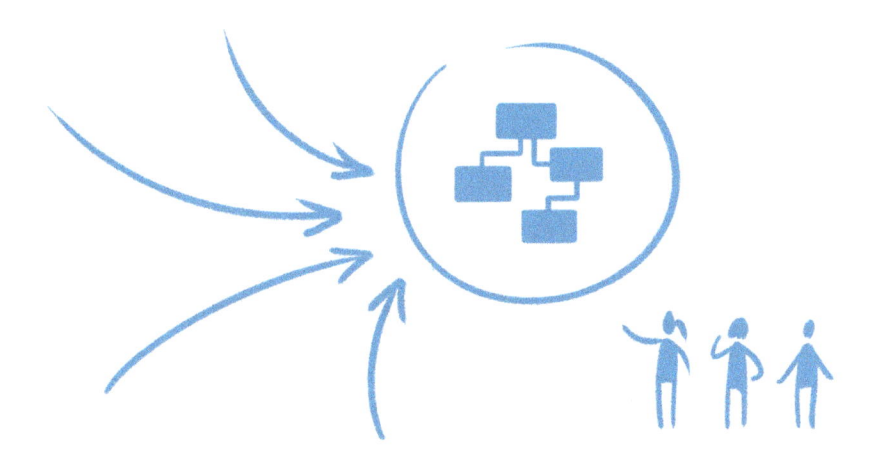

How will the leadership team and the board be set up?

What roles can and will different family members play as part of our philanthropic activities? What should the prerequisites for family involvement be?

What should our rules and processes of communication be? (Inside the family as well as beyond?) How visible do we want to be as a family?

How do we plan to involve the next generation?

Organization

Impact

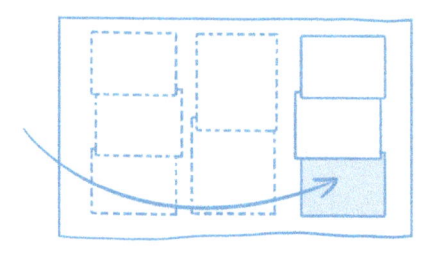

Setting the Scene

With the organization for your giving now in place, you are almost ready to set sail on your philanthropic voyage. But, before you get started, it is time to think about the final step in the *Family Philanthropy Navigator* – impact.

Impact is the effect your philanthropy has on the focus of your giving, your family and your partners, and the world. It is the reality of results compared with the hope of your ambitions. From the moment you start discussing the purpose of your giving with the outside world to engaging with partners and organizing your giving, you begin to have an impact. But what kind of impact will your philanthropic activities have?

How can you measure it and turn that assessment into action? How can you improve the chances of achieving your goals? Will your impact align with your ambitions? How can you assess progress along the way and adjust course if you need to?

The only way you can answer these questions is to start giving. Once you have taken that leap, you will be able to see the direct impact of your giving unfold. Depending on your selected cause, you will be able to witness the impact of your giving in the short term, in real time or only after a certain period of time has passed. Are things going according to plan or better than expected? Have you strayed off course? Are you sure you can avoid doing harm? Is it aligned with your purpose?

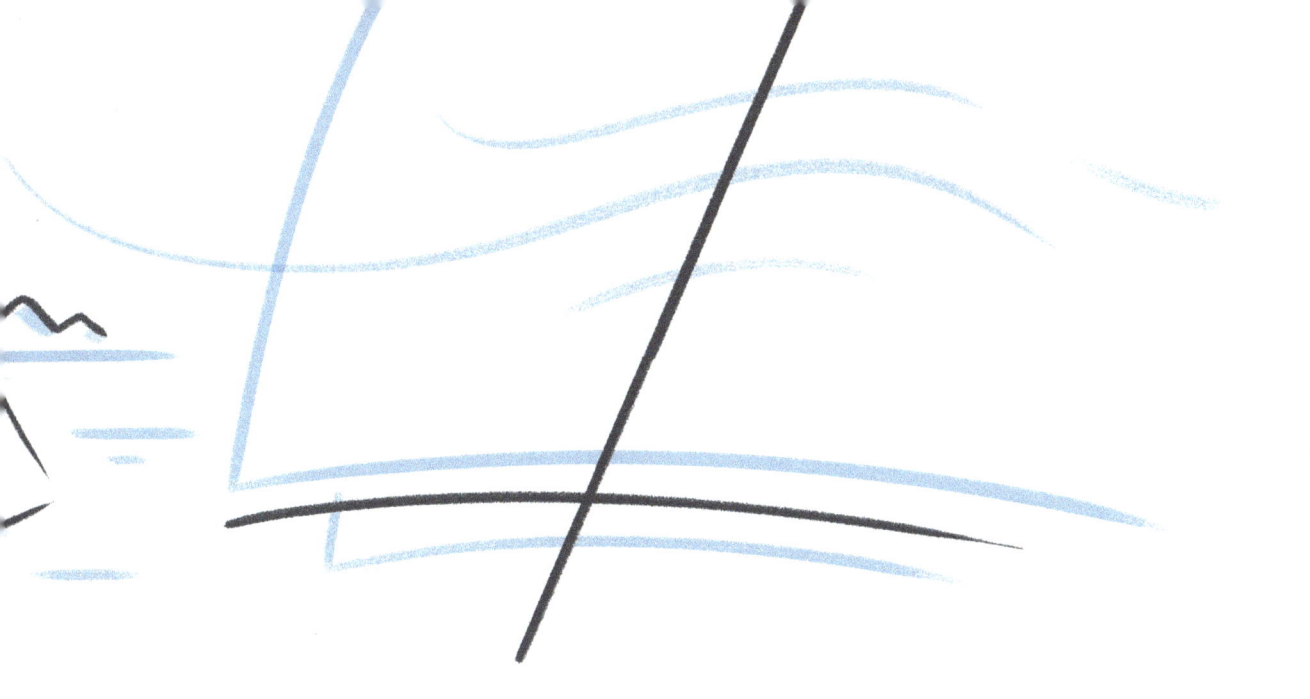

Insight

MONITORING AND EVALUATION

It is advisable to take a holistic and systemic approach to measuring impact. Family resources are at stake and, in the age of greater professionalism in philanthropy, it is important to provide yourself and your family with regular progress reports on all of your projects. Whatever information you collect, it can prove vital in informing your decisions. In this respect, you should understand the clear difference between ongoing monitoring and periodic evaluation. Often, evaluation is made before choosing a project or as you close the collaboration, while monitoring is carried out during the period of support.

	Monitoring	Evaluation
Frequency	Ongoing	Periodic
Coverage	All programs funded	Specific elements
Data	All beneficiaries	Sample
Cost	Distributed cost	Can be high
Application	Improvement	Basis for strategic decision

Impact   171

Organization

Philanthropy is not an exact science. Like any similarly ambitious undertaking that requires collaboration and coordination, it is a voyage riddled with variables and uncertainties, unexpected events and human error. Fine-tuning and taking stock are part and parcel of this journey.

The issues philanthropists address are often deeply rooted and complex – even more so in today's fast-paced and interconnected world. In order to have a real impact, philanthropy requires a lot of resources and the support and buy-in of a range of partners. Solutions to the world's greatest problems can no longer be addressed by one stakeholder alone, but instead require an orchestrated multistakeholder effort, which makes it increasingly complex for philanthropists to say, with certainty, what level of (positive) impact their giving might have. In practice, it is not always obvious that you may not achieve everything you set out to do. It may be that the outcomes are way off target, or just a little wayward.

It is important that you work in collaboration with your partners to define a plan and a process to achieve your mutual goals: reaching your ambition and creating long-lasting change. By taking time to deliberately and routinely focus on and plan your journey, while assessing the progress and holistic impact of your giving, you can understand where you are and what needs to change in your philanthropic model to improve your efforts.

Ultimately, if you want to improve the positive impact of your giving, you will need to compare what you expected to happen and what actually happened in practice. Can you get ahead and measure the positive or negative impact of your giving in your focus area or community? How has your giving affected the target and the environment?

You cannot achieve your desired impact overnight. It has to be embedded in your approach early on so that you have a clear baseline as you start your giving journey. In the words of Alan Lakein: *"Failing to plan is planning to fail."*

There is no best model to evaluate impact. Impact can be thought of and measured in many ways. It also depends on what you are trying to achieve. As a philanthropic family with the goal to not only positively influence a specific cause but also to unite the family, educate the next generation and transfer family values, and possibly even have a cohesive social impact strategy with your family business, you need to consider multiple dimensions of impact: for the cause, for the family or for the business.

Insight

OUTCOMES VS IMPACT

It can be helpful to distinguish between the concept of outcomes and the concept of impact. Outcomes and results are specific elements that you have targeted to achieve and that fall under the primary responsibility of the partners you support. Impact has broader implications. It encompasses the way your intervention affects the long-term picture, either directly or indirectly, either positively or negatively. For example, you can provide food to help address malnutrition in favelas by feeding a target number of recipients, but this action could be rendered useless in the long run if the root causes are not addressed. You may also stigmatize a group within the population. Making a lasting difference as a philanthropist often means looking at an issue in a holistic way and seeking solutions that can have a long-term impact. This might mean working with local organizations that have a different approach to solving your malnutrition challenge in the favelas, for example. When considering the impact of your giving, we recommend that you reflect on and explore how to make a sustainable difference in the world in conversation with the organization you support – as they often know the given context intimately.

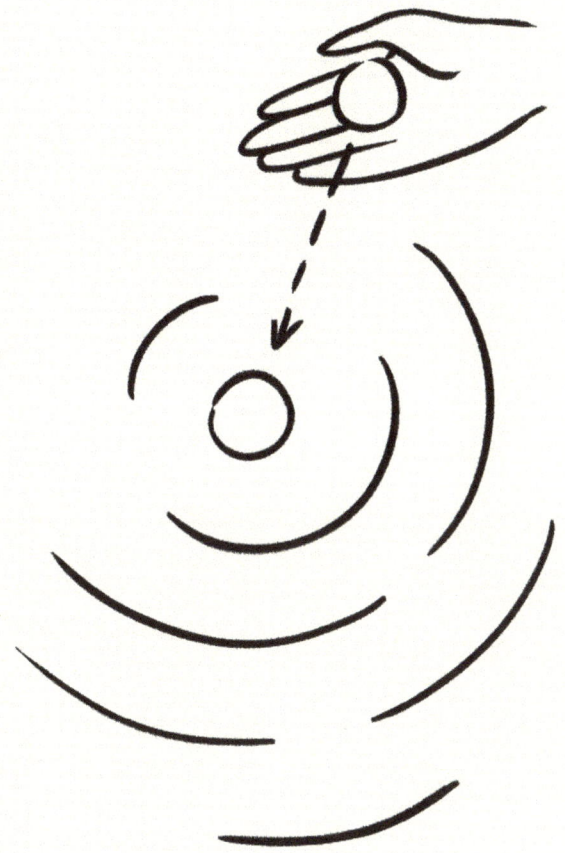

Impact   173

Organization

Knowing what you need to measure in your case, as well as what you can and cannot measure, is the first step in understanding impact as it relates to you and the partners you support. You can then start to think about how to measure it in coordination with your partners and then what to do with that information, both for you and for them.

You will most likely need to address some of the following questions: What kind of information or data do you need? Is it about specific numbers or more about storytelling, or both? What timeframes and frequency are you looking at? Do you need to be personally involved in the assessment, for example, by visiting projects? How can you progress while learning to improve your approach? Will your decision-making processes be linked to your data reports or benchmarks?

What you do with the data, in whatever form they come, is vital. As you begin, you may find yourself collecting a lot of data and anecdotes. But not all types of data are useful and the more data you have the more difficult it gets to "see the wood for the trees," make sense of them and come to meaningful conclusions. You will need to be crystal clear about what you wish to understand by collecting and analyzing data before you actually start collecting them. Philanthropy can use data to listen, learn and change course, to replicate best practice and models and to share knowledge.

The modern concept of sustainability can offer a helpful parallel for the philanthropist, using three dimensions – social, environmental and economic – to define your approach to assessing your impact. Within this, depending on your approach, it could be worthwhile to apply parameters to understand your impact, such as accuracy, efficacy, efficiency, cost, return on investment, risk or timelines.

From these measurements, over time, you could build up a set of lessons learned and best practices that can feed back into your purpose, relationships and organization to inform decision making and action. While this may not be appropriate for some, we would recommend that you approach your impact assessment with the same level of attention as you would give, for example, to the setup of your organization.

A thorough understanding of the nature of the impact you want to achieve and a thorough way to measure it will help you reach your goals in philanthropy, individually and as a family. It will provide relevant information to share with stakeholders, to set clear goals so that partners know what is expected and plan ahead, and to provide a constant stream of navigational data to keep you on course. But a word of warning: A sound approach to impact measurement requires working closely with the partners you support to make sure the process you set in place is of mutual benefit.

Impact is not just about data and information. It is about the whole journey and how you create long-lasting change for the beneficiaries. It is not just one photograph of a moment in time, it's a movie made up of thousands of frames. That means it is important to reflect and assess how you

Insight

STORIES AND DATA

There is value in collecting a range of information about the impact of your giving. While data can be fed back into the way you give to improve impact, they do not provide all the answers. As Albert Einstein said, *"Everything that can be counted does not necessarily count; everything that counts cannot necessarily be counted."* Anecdotal evidence and experience can be just as important in shaping your philanthropic journey. While the right data are vital, there can rarely be any substitute for a compelling real-world story or qualitative indicator that tells you about how your giving has changed a life, or not quite met expectations. A combination of data and stories is often the best approach.

engage with others in your ecosystem of giving, for example, from board members to partners in the field.

Indeed, a responsible donor needs to balance a certain level of explicit and implicit expectations while trusting in their partners to handle adversity. Finding the right balance will enable you to act in a more predictable way and give your partners sufficient freedom to act while being accountable for what really matters. Having the tools and processes to measure impact is a good way of providing guidance and setting expectations.

While a certain degree of control provides useful parameters for partners to operate in, you should be careful to avoid being too overbearing. It may be helpful to balance your ambitions with a humble acceptance that you do not have all the answers and that things can go wrong. In giving, everyone is a partner focused on achieving long-lasting change.

In this chapter, we will take you through ways of thinking about and measuring the impact of your giving to ensure you can be as effective as possible, and equipped to adapt as circumstances evolve. Ultimately, you will be able to answer and act on the following questions:

→ What is the desired impact of our giving?
→ How do we know we have achieved it?

Impact   175

Organization

Setting the Compass

To help you explore the idea of impact in giving, we have chosen the following trade-offs around the topic. By reflecting on each of these areas, you will be able to come to an understanding of what impact means for you and how you can incorporate it in your activities, assess results and optimize your giving.

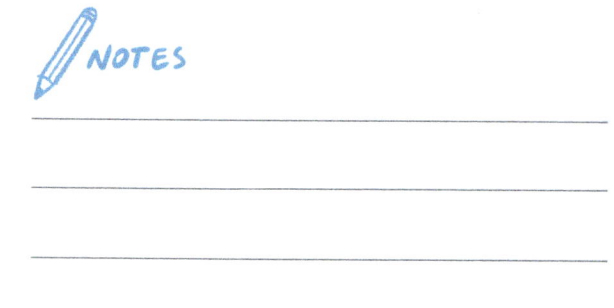

NOTES

QUALITATIVE DATA ————|————|————|————|————|———— QUALITATIVE INFORMATION

Collecting and analyzing data to assess impact from a quantitative perspective

Data can provide a wealth of information to guide and shape the way you give. But data only tell part of the story. For instance, if you provide support to girls to improve access to secondary schools, reduce dropout rates and to help them become self-confident young women, the quantitative data you collect can tell you how many do well in their exams, how many attend classes and what they do next. However, qualitative information gives you insights beyond the numbers – it can tell you whether they are more aware of their rights or are healthier and happier. In that sense, qualitative indicators can play an important role in measuring your impact.

Measuring how you are doing from a qualitative perspective

→ What kind of **information** do you need to assess the **impact** of your giving?
→ How important are **data** such as **KPIs**?
→ Are you more interested in **stories** and **qualitative** information?
→ Would it be helpful to receive a **blend of both**?

SELF-EVALUATION ⊢—┼—┼—┼—┼—┼—┼—┼—⊣ **EXTERNAL EVALUATION**

Setting up and conducting own evaluation of your giving

The main purpose of an evaluation is to observe if your support is effective, efficient, relevant and producing desired results. Taking the example of the girls from the previous trade-off, if you want to evaluate your giving internally, it will require you or your staff to be neutral in order to understand where and how to improve the way you support those young female students. An external resource might be able to take a step back and take a different view on the most effective way to manage the relationship between you and your giving partner. There are advantages to both approaches, and you may find it useful to combine both, to do, for example, a more frequent self-evaluation and an occasional more detailed external assessment, perhaps every one to three years.

Relying on outside help to assess progress

→ Do you want to and – can you – run **diagnostics** and **evaluation** in-house?
→ Would it be more appropriate to **outsource** evaluating to **external experts**?
→ Do you want to combine **both approaches**?

✏️ **NOTES**

_____
_____
_____
_____

Organization

FUNDING ACTIVITIES ├┼┼┼┼┼┼┼┼┤ **FUNDING RESULTS**

Providing support to fund activities without setting clear, expected outcomes

Many philanthropists focus on funding results and, therefore, they define and strive towards achieving very specific outcomes. However, funding activities without specifying an end goal can become necessary when it is more challenging to predict outcomes. Let's stick to our example of the girls gaining greater access to education. You could fund continuous teacher training, provide student materials for schools and possibly scholarships. You could certainly measure all of those activities, alongside students' attendance in classes, but if your ambition is to make sure you get specific results, you could set targets for how many girls pass their final exams and how many continue their education, both of which will be tangible outcomes. However, the additional impact of girls staying in school may include having children at an older age, having smaller families and enjoying better health.

Setting out clear, specific goals and defining impact for your giving

→ Do you want to measure the **direct results** of your funding?
→ Are you more focused on **specifics** or the **bigger picture**?
→ Do you want to understand the **broader outcome** of your **support**?

NOTES

_____

_____

_____

Family Philanthropy Navigator

SUPPORTING ORGANIZATION ONLY ←——————————→ **SUPPORTING BENEFICIARIES DIRECTLY**

Structuring your giving to support the work of organization(s) only

Organizing your giving to directly support beneficiaries only

Take some time to reflect on whether you will focus your concept of successful impact on supporting an organization or the direct, specific improvement of final beneficiaries. This will have implications for how you measure your impact and how you adjust your approach to reach your goals. In recent years, venture philanthropy has developed an approach for investing primarily in organizations. Funders not only provide finance, but they also sit on boards and support capacity building. On the other side, some donors are much more cautious about investing in an organization's development. They value, above all, a greater portion of their grants finding its way to beneficiaries and are very wary about the amount that goes to administration. At an extreme level, this may mean supporting beneficiaries directly.

→ Are you interested in supporting the **work** and **development** of an organization?
→ Do you want to focus solely on the **direct support** of your **beneficiaries**?
→ Does it make sense to adopt a **blended** or **varied approach** over time?

NOTES

_____

_____

_____

Impact

Organization

Activities

It is our recommendation that you consider impact as an ongoing element of your giving that needs to be measured, adjusted and fed back into your giving structure and purpose so that you can move closer to achieving your goals.

Having successfully defined the purpose (the why and what), the relationships (the who) and the organization (how) of your giving you can now put together your impact strategy. The following activities will help you get started with this.

Family Philanthropy Navigator Questions:

→ What is the desired impact of our giving?
→ How do we know that we have achieved it?

**Activity 1:
Review Your Trade-Offs**

Step 1

Review the various trade-offs presented earlier in this chapter and, individually, answer the following questions. Use different colors to highlight your response to the two questions as they relate to each of the trade-offs. You can position yourself anywhere along the spectrum, from one end to the other.

1. **Where is our philanthropy today?**
2. **Where would I like our philanthropy to be in the future?**

Step 2

As a family, compare and discuss where each one of you marked dots for "where are we today" and "where would we like to be". What are the similarities and differences? Where are you aligned or not? How can this further shape your journey?

Step 3

If there are any differences in your perspectives, discuss how you wish to address these.

* Note to aspiring philanthropists:
If you are not yet philanthropically active you can simply focus on question 2 in Step 1.

Organization

Activity 2:
Measure, Monitor Your Giving

Step 1

Review the Elements You Have Defined in the Previous Chapters

As a first step, revisit the other aspects of your philanthropy by going back to the Purpose and Relationships sections as well as the Resources and Governance chapters in this section of the book. Make sure you've addressed the following five questions as they will form the basis for the following steps.

1. What is the focus of our giving?
2. What are our ambitions?
3. What is our desired outcome and what are our metrics of success?
4. What type and amount of resources do we provide?
5. What is our timeframe to achieve the desired outcome?

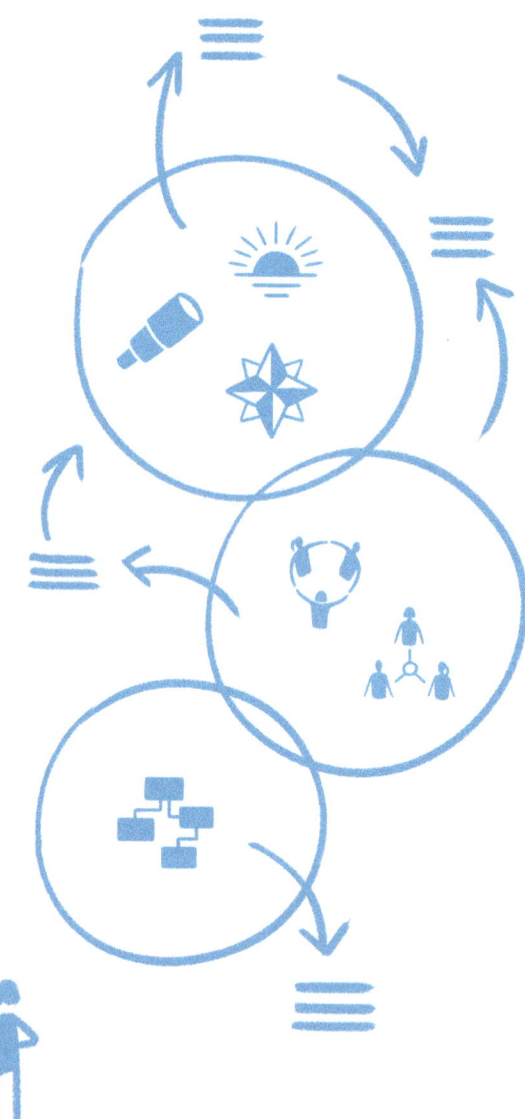

182 Family Philanthropy Navigator

Step 2

Define a Process for Monitoring and Collecting Data

Once you have answered these questions, think about a process to collect the necessary data/information to take informed decisions. Reflect on the following questions, then discuss and agree on these points as a family. It might make sense to already include your partners in this step as you will, ultimately, need to agree on this process together.

> 1. What types of data are we, as philanthropists, interested in receiving?
> 2. What are our sources of data and information?
> 3. How will we be interacting with our partners in order to gather these data?
> 4. In what frequency would we like to receive and review these data?
> 5. In what format and through which process would you like to monitor the impact of your giving?
> 6. Who is ultimately responsible for this inside the family or our philanthropic organization?

In case you are engaged in a range of philanthropic activities or are supporting a number of different causes, it is advisable to go through these questions for each one of them separately, as the type, source, frequency and format of data collection and monitoring will differ depending on what you are focusing on and where.

We recommend that your choices about these various points become an integral part of your formal agreement with the partner or implementing organization. This clarifies positions and expectations and removes any unnecessary ambiguity. It will also help your partner provide you with the necessary information in a structured manner.

Organization

Step 3

Decide On How to Use the Data for Monitoring and Evaluation

Impact is a key element in the final stage of monitoring and evaluation. After you have started your giving you will want to review and evaluate the effectiveness and efficiency of your giving. You, your family and your giving partners will want to assess whether your giving led to the desired outcomes or whether you need to make certain adjustments. Reviewing and analyzing the data you previously collected will help you answer the following questions.

1. Have we achieved what we wanted to achieve?
2. Do we close down the support or do we continue?
3. What is working and what isn't working?
4. Should we adjust our support, reassess the partners we work with or change our giving strategy?
5. What can we communicate with others to help improve philanthropy overall?

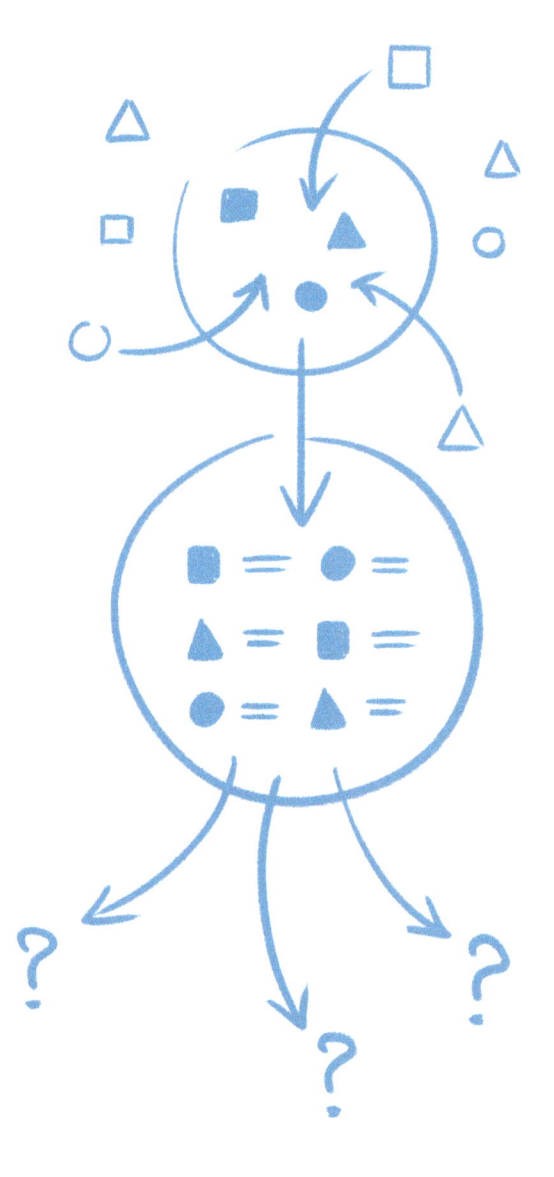

In this step, it is important to decide what you do with the information as well as with the final results. As suggested, you can decide to close down the project, if originally intended. You can decide to renew it on a similar footing to make sure you can enhance or continue the great work of your giving partners. You could also decide to share your learnings with peer philanthropists or gather a community of similar giving partners that might not know each other. After all, communicating experiences and know-how are core components of the greater mission of philanthropy as we seek to make a positive difference in the world together. Philanthropy produces value for the whole of society. If you have insight and experience to communicate, it is important to make time to reflect on those learnings and how best to share them so that our partners, peers and society can benefit.

As we will explore in the subsequent Learning section, giving is a continuous cycle of learning and improving. Hence, a clear-cut process to measure your impact is crucial. Along the way, you might twist and tweak a number of dimensions in your *Family Philanthropy Navigator*.

Organization

Case Study
Fark Holding

In Conversation with Ahu Büyükkuşoğlu Serter

"Think in terms of the 'total happiness effect' that your giving can create."

→ **Name:** Ahu Büyükkuşoğlu Serter, President, Fark Holding; Founder, Arya Women Investment Platform; Founder, Fark Labs R&D and Innovation Center

→ **Country of origin:** Turkey

→ **Family size (total number of family members):**
Seven in total: two brothers and their five children (the 1st and the 2nd generation)

→ **Background information about your family's legacy and current business activities:**
Two brothers started the business in 1968. Today, the family holding owns 10 companies in various sectors: automotive, white goods, tourism, construction, and R&D. We employ 2,500 people with annual revenues of 250 million EUR. Our family business motto is: "Better future together."

→ **Which generation are you part of?**
2nd generation

→ **Number of family members involved in your philanthropic activities:**
All family members contribute.

186 Family Philanthropy Navigator

Areas of giving

Focus of Giving
Our areas of focus are:
1. Art
2. Diversity
3. Education
4. Female empowerment

Country/Region
We give in Turkey.

Other Aspects Worth Noting
Our family's philanthropic ventures are independent entities that receive seed capital from the family holding and its companies. For example, in 2012, we established a social venture called the Arya Women Investment Platform. Through its investors, the platform invests "smart money" in female-led businesses. In loving memory of my mother Fatoş Büyükkuşoğlu, and to recognize the leadership potential of women in Turkey, every year we provide a scholarship to distinguish exceptional women from our region who have proven their leadership.
In addition, in 2019, one of our businesses was recognized by TAİDER - an association of family-owned businesses - for its excellence in supporting women in the workplace called "POLARIS - Kuzey Yıldızı" Sustainability Award.

Structure of giving

Type of Structure
The family can give in two ways: (1) individually; (2) though the family holding. The formal giving vehicle is integrated in the holding's governance structure.

Family Governance/Decision-Making
Philanthropy discussions happen at the level of the family council and our Social Philanthropy Committee. Plans for giving are developed and discussed three years in advance.

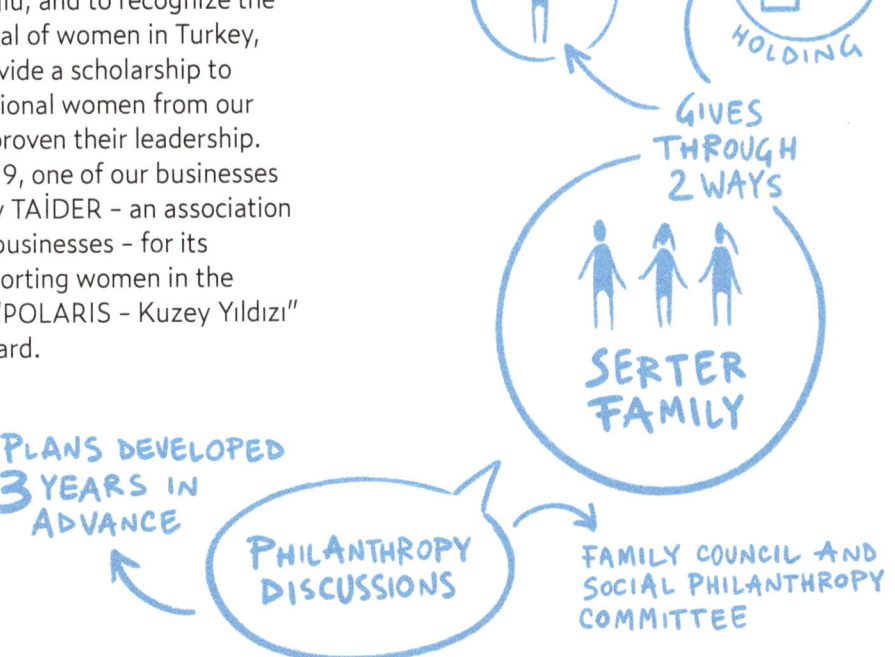

Case Studies

Organization

Navigator Questions

Resources

→ **What do we give? What do we need? How do we fill the gaps?**
We have a very hands-on approach. We execute all our own projects. We recognize that resources in philanthropy can be very scarce and, as a result, we are very results-oriented and entrepreneurial in the way we invest our own resources and execute projects. Family members can use reserved capital to support various philanthropic projects. The portions of giving correspond to the number of shares that both branches own (70 vs 30 percent). The philanthropic budget is renewed each year.

To fill gaps, we seek funds from external sponsors who become co-owners of our philanthropic entities. Our philanthropic entities are designed to attract investments from other philanthropists who care about the same causes.

Governance

→ **How do we structure our giving? What rules, processes and policies help us?**
There are two funds: (1) dedicated to personal causes; (2) a fund run by the holding company with the oversight by the Social Philanthropy Committee. The Social Philanthropy Committee consists of two family members, the HR Director of the Holding and the Director of Corporate Relations. The committee reports to the holding's board. The holding company contributes 0.5% of EBITDA to the annual philanthropy budget. All decisions are first approved by the committee. This model allows for agility. The holding company or its 10 companies can support any philanthropic project approved by the respective board. Then, we create independent philanthropic entities to organize them. Our philanthropic entities sign flexible contracts with each of the sponsor companies. Each company can withdraw support for any philanthropic entity, depending on its performance or changes in circumstances.

All family members are invited to present ideas for giving projects. Our rule is that projects need to be related to the focus of family or business giving. Family members need to pitch the business case for their projects. All projects are expected to become standalone and self-sustaining. The family provides seed capital and acts as an enabler. The approach is to be an entrepreneur in philanthropy.

For some projects, it is more challenging to become financially self-sustaining. For example, my family is building a museum for our art collection. To ensure that it will be self-sustaining, we plan to build or invest in an additional venture that could feed in financial resources to the museum.

Impact

→ **What is the desired impact of our giving? How do we know that we have achieved it?**

Our family has evolved from a focus on business to a more vision- and goal-oriented approach: a family with a purpose. Today, business is only a tool to make our lives and the lives of our communities better.

We are closely tracking the impact of all our projects; and, depending on each project, we measure and monitor very specific KPIs. For example, in relation to our social venture called the ARYA Women's Investment Platform, we measure the following: the number of female entrepreneurs selected, the number of countries represented, the number of investors we engaged with, the number of companies that have changed their settings to a more female-friendly working environment after working with us. However, for some projects, it may be more challenging to measure their impact. In these cases, we carefully listen to our beneficiaries. For example, in relation to the New-Generation Library, founded by my father, we received feedback from the local community that came back to us saying: "Your library has changed our lives for better." We also noticed that other communities have started to imitate this library-project, and we were very glad to see that our idea was spreading and impacting so many other lives.

KEY LEARNINGS AND RECOMMENDATIONS

1. **Be open and learn from others.** Learn from others who have tried to achieve or have achieved what you are trying to do. You don't have to invent something new all the time, finding the ones who have done it before and partnering with them can also lead to success.

2. **Give now.** You don't have to be a very rich family to be active in philanthropy. There are many ways to give. Philanthropy is a journey, and it should become an integral part of the family and the business.

3. **Be accountable.** Acknowledge that you are responsible not only for yourself but also the society you live in. Therefore, it is essential that in your philanthropic work you bring together also other stakeholders in order to pursue your mutual goals and to create a sense of a shared purpose.

4. **Measure but don't get obsessed.** Care about your key success indicators but don't make them your end goal. Think in terms of the "total happiness effect" that your giving can create. Sometimes you start with a hunch, but you don't know how to measure it. If you are obsessed with measuring things, it can stifle your ability to get started. You have to have a vision and work towards it. Metrics come later, when you are scaling your purpose or goal.

5. **Be creative and dream big.** Everything starts with a dream. It doesn't start with resources. You have to learn to dream independent of what you have and work hard to get there, and to increase your resources to reach that dream.

Case Studies

Organization

Case Study
Fondation Philanthropique NEXT

In Conversation with Thierry Mauvernay and Cédric Mauvernay

> "Providing the funds is not enough. We need to remain responsible and ensure that they are used properly."

→ **Name:** Thierry and Cédric Mauvernay, Foundation Philanthropique NEXT (FPN), Debiopharm

→ **Country of origin:** Switzerland

→ **Family size (total number of family members):**
G2: Thierry and Nadine Mauvernay
G3: Cédric and Anna Mauvernay

→ **Background information about your family's legacy and current business activities:**
Our family business, the Debiopharm Group, was founded in 1979 in Lausanne, Switzerland. We have two branches in our group: a life science arm with biopharmaceutical companies active in drug development, manufacturing proprietary drugs, diagnostics, and an asset management arm composed of real estate, Private Equity, direct participations, among other things.

→ **Which generation are you part of?**
2nd and 3rd generation

→ **Number of family members involved in your philanthropic activities:** Three.

Family Philanthropy Navigator

Areas of giving

Focus of Giving
FPN focuses on education, immigration, extreme poverty and autism and the Fondation d'Aide d'Urgence for people in distress, including the group's staff in difficult situations.

Country/Region
We are active in Cambodia, Vietnam, Lebanon, Indonesia, South Africa, Tanzania, Bolivia, Switzerland.

Structure of giving

Type of Structure
We have two foundations: a corporate foundation called Fondation d'Aide d'Urgence and a family foundation called Fondation Philanthropique NEXT. In addition, we give directly through the company.

Family Governance/Decision-Making
Thierry sits on the board of the two foundations. Other family members are active only in the family foundation. There is a clear distinction between corporate and family giving.

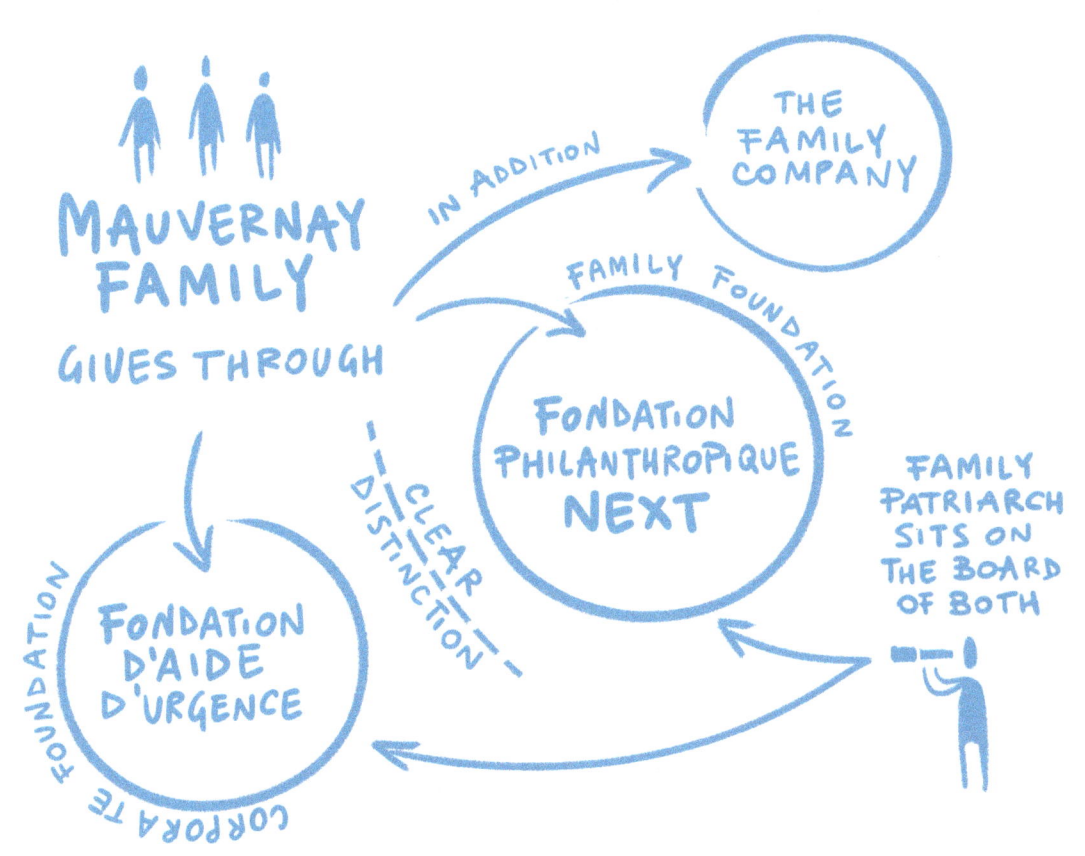

Organization

Navigator Questions

Resources

→ **What do we give? What do we need? How do we fill the gaps?**
We make donations through the family foundation to develop concrete projects. Our family is actively engaged in selecting projects, setting targets and monitoring impact. Today, we are also directly active in the creation of an ecosystem to help autistic people in Switzerland. We actively seek implementing partners for our projects. These partnerships are fairly long-term and last for about three to six years. Regarding the Fondation d'Aide d'Urgence we directly help individuals rather than projects.

Governance

→ **How do we structure our giving? What rules, processes and policies help us?**
Our business-related giving is organized through a corporate foundation where Thierry (the group's president), the companies' CEO, an HR representative, and a lawyer sit on the board. Our corporate foundation receives a designated amount per employee per year from each company within the group.

Our family foundation has a "family-only" board composed of Nadine, Thierry and Cédric. The foundation has a part-time employee solely in charge of the autism project and receives the support of trusted philanthropy advisors. All decisions are made and approved by the respective boards. This giving is not related to the business but solely our family's interests. Our family Foundation Philanthropique NEXT is funded through a percentage of the company's annual profits. However, the foundation is financially self-sustaining, having set aside a portion of capital in order to cover the financial needs of the foundation for a period of at least 3 years. This allows to foundation to be less dependent on the financial performance of the business and, as a result, enables the foundation to operate even in difficult times. Board members know their giving partners well and meet them regularly.

Impact

→ **What is the desired impact of our giving? How do we know that we have achieved it?**
We recognize that creating impact takes time. Therefore, our foundation tends to support a smaller number of organizations over a number of years. For each of our projects, we select the organization first and then we agree on a joint strategy to achieve impact. This involves the definition of specific targets for each project in order to know if our giving is aligned with our purpose and how successful a specific project is. We sign a commitment and a contract for the duration of the project. Our support runs for a clearly defined period of

time and our objective is to help each organization to achieve the next step in their development. Data, reports and field visits are important elements in our decision making.

We leverage others' knowledge and expertise in our own giving. Our model is to acquire expertise and knowledge from external resources. We do not want to "reinvent the wheel." For example, we organize events where experts and important organizations can showcase their best practices and share ways to achieve impact. The autism project is a little different in that we become actors and promote and create actions.

KEY LEARNINGS AND RECOMMENDATIONS

1. **Be committed and follow-up.** Work on projects and follow the achievements. Be committed and professional at each stage of your giving and make sure that you follow-up with your recipients. You can achieve real impact in the long-term by making sure that you, your family, and partners do good and do it well.

2. **Keep improving.** Maintain the passion and commitment and keep improving your family's organization of giving to reflect the family's purpose and match the needs of your beneficiaries.

3. **Make your philanthropic investment relevant.** Think IMPACT, be efficient. To achieve a desired impact or de-risk a philanthropic investment, you will need to integrate due diligence and follow-up processes to monitor how your money is spent. As a donor, you have a responsibility to ensure that your money is spent in the most effective and efficient way.

4. **Be an engaged donor.** Providing money is not enough. Be flexible and engaged, take responsibility – have an open discussion with your partners, try to understand their needs and their goals, and work together when selecting programs and defining your targets. It is highly advisable that you also visit your projects on site. It is a great opportunity to "touch the reality," reflect and learn and show your interest in your partners.

Case Studies   193

Organization

Case Study
Ishk Tolaram Foundation

In Conversation with Sumitra Aswani

"Put the beneficiary at the center of your decision making."

→ **Name:** Sumitra Aswani, Board member and Executive Director of Ishk Tolaram Foundation

→ **Country of origin:** India/Indonesia

→ **Family size (total number of family members):** 48 (Family Assembly)

→ **Background information about your family's legacy and current business activities:**
Our business started in 1948 in Indonesia. Today, it is mostly engaged in fast-moving consumer goods and services in emerging markets within Africa, Indonesia and Estonia.

→ **Which generation are you part of?**
4th generation (from the founder)

→ **Number of family members involved in your philanthropic activities:**
Five family members are actively involved in philanthropic activities through Ishk Tolaram Foundation: three in leadership roles and three on the foundation board. I play a dual role. That is, I am the Executive Director of the foundation and also a board member. Other family members engage in personal philanthropic activites that run alongside the foundation.

Areas of giving

Focus of Giving
We focus on three areas: education, healthcare, and skills training.

Country/Region
We are active in Singapore, Nigeria, and Indonesia, and have just started operations in Estonia.

Other Aspects Worth Noting
We have had various iterations of our philanthropy, and Ishk Tolaram Foundation is the latest and most central version so far. This foundation was set up to fulfill the founder's (of the foundation) desire to put philanthropy and giving back at the center of our family's purpose. In 2015, the family business Tolaram Group was restructured as a trust with Ishk Tolaram Foundation becoming the single largest beneficiary of the family trust. As part of this restructuring, we have improved our business and family governance with a family council, assembly, and constitution.

Structure of giving

Type of Structure
Ishk Tolaram Foundation was established in 2016. It is both an operational and grant-making foundation. We give grants to projects directly and run our own programs.

Family Governance/Decision-Making
Our foundation's board consists of four board members. Three are family members from different generations, and one is an independent director. The majority of the foundation's board and the chairman of the board must be drawn from the family as per the current charter.

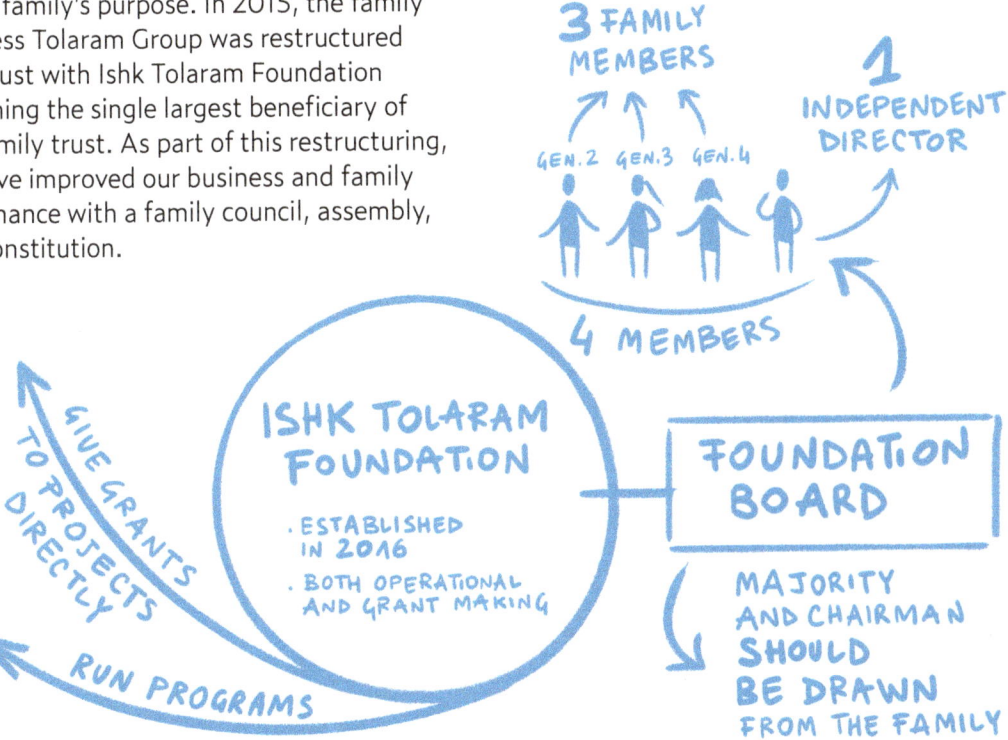

Case Studies 195

Organization

Navigator Questions

Resources

→ **What do we give? What do we need? How do we fill the gaps?**
The foundation receives income from the family trust. We evaluate and disburse grants and also develop and run our own programs. To identify gaps, we combine our research with going into the field to talk with beneficiaries and understand their needs. Then, we assess what resources we can and cannot provide, and from there identify the additional resources we need. Finally, we bring together resources and relevant partners with special expertise and skills.

Our projects are usually run in collaboration with partners. These partnerships are very program-specific and range from government, to non-profits, to private sector organizations. Some business employees also lend their expertise and time in advising the foundation on its activities.

Governance

→ **How do we structure our giving? What rules, processes and policies help us?**
Family members are involved in the foundation as part of the board of directors. We have entities in four countries (Singapore, Nigeria, Indonesia, and Estonia) where we give. Each of the countries is overseen by a member of the team. Presently, Indonesia and Singapore are helmed by family members. These entities report to the executive director, who is currently a family member, and the board of the main foundation in Singapore. Internally, we have set up governance policies such as who can serve on the board, how and when the board should be renewed, and what its responsibilities are. Each of our entities also complies with national laws and regulations.

Impact

→ **What is the desired impact of our giving? How do we know that we have achieved it?**
We work to achieve impact within the areas of our focus to benefit the communities around us and learn from them as well. To do this, we regularly review our programs and iterate on various program components to ensure that they are meeting their objectives, are relevant to the needs of our communities and are in line with the founder's wishes. We monitor and evaluate the impact of our programs through continual engagement and feedback. We collect data on the number of lives that our various programs have impacted, as well as qualitative data to help us understand the depth of impact. We produce and publish annual reports in which we describe all our activities and impact. For example, in 2017, the Ishk Limb Centre reported having impacted 10,719 lives, and, by 2019, this had increased to 14,613 individuals.

KEY LEARNINGS AND RECOMMENDATIONS

1. **Context is everything.** Having an idea means nothing if you can't contextualize it to what is relevant to the communities you are trying to serve, including taking into account the local geography, culture and politics.

2. **Beneficiaries, beneficiaries, beneficiaries.** Putting the beneficiary at the center of your decision-making, being as professional as possible, and bringing in the right resources will go a long way towards helping you minimize mistakes.

3. **Customize your giving.** There are many ways to give and it is OK that "one size doesn't fit all." Be flexible to cater for the different interests of your family and consider other philanthropic structures such as donor-advised funds, or other means of giving. A more customized way of giving can help you achieve greater impact, especially if you outsource some of this to seasoned experts.

4. **Know your ecosystem.** Leverage your philanthropic ecosystem and exchange with others to accelerate your learning rather than trying out all these learnings yourself.

5. **Learn from professionals.** Bring in philanthropy experts to leverage their experience and expertise to help you professionalize and accelerate your giving. The fallout of a poorly planned program can be significant, and you will want to avoid these negative consequences where possible.

TERRA INCOGNITA

Learning

204 **Activity**

Learning

Introduction

Are you really making a difference with your giving?

Are you still focusing on the right cause or is it time to change course? Have the needs of the ultimate beneficiaries changed over time? Are you giving to the right organization? Are the other members of your family still committed? Do you have the right partners to implement your giving? Could you change something to have greater impact? How do you learn from your experiences so that you can, over time, improve your giving?

This final section will explore and describe how to embrace the notion of learning within your giving journey so that you can continue to build and maintain an effective and healthy philanthropic organization.

Learning plays a crucial role in philanthropy. There are many different ways to learn, and we all have our preferences. There are a number of variations to consider when it comes to learning:

1. Learning can happen in the moment or it can happen reflectively. Both ways of learning can be a valuable source of insights and knowledge in philanthropy.
2. Learning can happen by acquiring new knowledge in a conceptual manner, or it can happen "on the job." In philanthropy, "learning by doing" has proven to be one of the most effective and efficient ways to continuously improve.
3. Learning can happen alone or with others. As much as we learn from our own mistakes and successes, we also learn from those who have embarked on this journey before us. However, for various reasons, many families decide to be discreet about their philanthropic giving, which can make sharing with and learning from others tricky.

Which activities are truly value adding and which ones could be discontinued or improved? Value addition in philanthropy doesn't necessarily come from the simple act of giving money. Instead, it is the combination of allocating the right types and amounts of resources to the cause or causes you are passionate about with the support of the most qualified people and partners. When these various components and stakeholders come together, you can achieve true value creation.

No philanthropist can get all these factors right from the beginning but, through careful learning and reflection, it is possible to understand why certain aspects of your giving might have been suboptimal and what improvements you could make.

Insight

THINK RENEWAL

Any organization has its life cycle – from creation to termination. This is no different for philanthropy. Across this cycle, families must manage the operational challenges of establishing or running a philanthropic organization, such as asset control, startup costs, management and administrative costs, and taxes. Beyond this, there are other challenges to be met and overcome, for example, a diminishing family interest in a cause due to dispersed multigenerational interests or maybe, over time, the focus of your giving might become less important. Being prepared to renew your philanthropic organization while instilling a spirit of continuous learning and improvement will help to ensure your giving remains relevant and effective. Our experience shows that motivations often remain consistent over generations but priorities, like preferences, can change.

Introduction

Learning

Linking Learning to the Navigator

Learning can trigger a pivot within any of the eight dimensions of the *Family Philanthropy Navigator*, whether it's the purpose of your giving, the family and non-family stakeholders you wish to involve or the organizational setup of your giving. We recommend that you regard and adopt the concept of learning as an integral, fluid and continuous part of your philanthropic journey – rather than as a separate activity that only happens when something goes wrong or at a specific time of year. Learning should be embedded in each of the steps of the navigator, and then made permanent as an ongoing component of your philanthropic activities and reflections.

Some key questions you might want to ask yourself:

> → How can we create a culture of learning inside the family as well as inside our philanthropic activity?
> → How can we ensure that those involved in our philanthropic journey – both family and partners – fully embrace a learning mindset? How can we learn together?
> → How can we improve learning from others while, at the same time, act as a role model and share our experience?
> → How can we connect learning with the evaluation of our giving?

For novice philanthropists, it will be helpful to integrate learning as a key element from the very beginning so that it becomes part of your culture of giving and you can learn and improve as you go. You will want to think about how, today and in the future, you will want to systematically embrace the notion of learning to ensure that you are on the right track or, if not, how you want to adjust the course.

In the early stages of your philanthropic journey, it is important that you remain flexible and show a willingness to learn and adjust. That way you can gradually professionalize your giving and ensure that you have a positive impact.

Exchanging with and learning from more advanced philanthropists is a great way to start. Don't shy away from speaking with other families in your network and openly asking them about their approach to philanthropy, what their learnings have been and what advice they might have for you.

For more established philanthropists, the exercise of completing the navigator and assessing whether you wish to make any changes to one or more dimensions of the navigator is already an act of reflection and learning.

Over time, you may want to consider incorporating a more formal and regular way of learning for the future, which could include a regular review of the core dimensions of the *Family Philanthropy Navigator*. You might want to specify a mechanism for, and the frequency of, a more formal review process and any learning activities.

Building a Learning Culture and Organization

Philanthropists and their organizations engage in learning for a variety of reasons. First of all, learning helps them become more effective and efficient and, as a result, they can do more for their ultimate beneficiaries. Moreover, they leverage learning as a vehicle to foster dialogue and exchange within the family, with their philanthropic staff as well as with their partners.

Learning is also a great way to shape and refine your giving strategy. Instead of trying to think of the most effective and efficient way to give, you can engage with the ecosystem around you to come up with better ideas, test your ideas as well as shape and refine them. By establishing a learning culture and organization, you can also ensure that it's acceptable for everyone that you go back and constructively review some of your ongoing activities and shape the path forward. Ultimately, learning is a critical way of thinking and working when it comes to assessing the outcomes of projects you have completed.

Learning is essential for every philanthropic family and should be leveraged strategically in order to learn across generations. Learning is equally important when you consider your partnership network as well as the beneficiaries you try to help with your giving. Actively involving them in your thought processes will not only lead to more creative and, mostly, relevant approaches to giving, but also signal to them that you truly care about their work.

Learning Together with Your Family and Your Partners

For a philanthropic family, it is of critical importance that learning becomes an integral part of the family's values and activities. Being curious, inquisitive and open to new knowledge and experience makes a difference when a family wants to ensure that their giving leads to their desired results. Also, many families leverage philanthropy as a vehicle for collective learning, across generations. It is a fun and engaging way for families to learn together; when scouting for causes or partners, or going on field trips to visit beneficiary partners.

Setting up a culture for learning is often handled through existing governance functions such as the family council and can also be supported through the family office. The senior generation in the family, as well as the leadership team of the philanthropic initiative, need to signal a willingness and a commitment to learning. This is critical so that the next generation grows into this way of thinking and working from the beginning.

If you plan to engage your family over generations in giving, the ability of each generation to learn and renew your organization will be crucial to achieving sustainable philanthropic success. Make sure that all family members get a chance to voice their ideas and opinions because not doing so might lead to tensions within the family. You might need to also revisit your family governance and how your family vision, mission and values translate into your giving.

Introduction

Learning

Activity

In the following activity, we will share a few initial questions you can ask yourself when it comes to evaluating your philanthropy. While this is primarily targeted towards established philanthropists, we still advise aspiring philanthropists to review this list carefully as it will help you shape your journey moving forward.

Clearly, this is only the beginning of a more thorough and in-depth learning process, but it is important to get started. This activity is closely linked to the eight dimensions of the *Family Philanthropy Navigator*, and you and your family should carefully go through each of those steps and have a detailed conversation about what has worked well, what could be improved and, most importantly, what necessary changes you will be making moving forward.

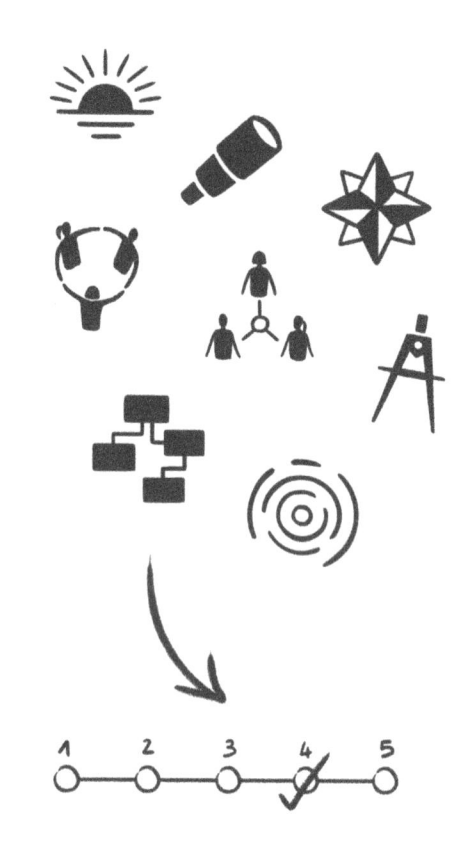

Step 1

Review the eight dimensions of the *Family Philanthropy Navigator* and assess each of them by rating them from 1–5.

Theme/dimension in the navigator	Questions	1 Strongly disagree	2 Disagree	3 Neutral	4 Agree	5 Strongly agree
PURPOSE	The purpose of our giving is clearly defined and provides the necessary direction to our work.	1	2	3	4	5
Motivation	We are strongly motivated to be philanthropically engaged.	1	2	3	4	5
Motivation	The reason(s) for our continued philanthropic giving have not changed.	1	2	3	4	5
Focus	The cause(s) we are passionate about have not changed.	1	2	3	4	5
Focus	We have alignment across the family when it comes to the causes to support.	1	2	3	4	5
Ambition	It is clear to everybody in our family what philanthropic success means to us.	1	2	3	4	5
Ambition	Our goals and metrics of success have not changed.	1	2	3	4	5

Activity

Learning

Theme/dimension in the navigator	Questions	1 Strongly disagree	2 Disagree	3 Neutral	4 Agree	5 Strongly agree
RELATIONSHIPS	We have clearly defined the relationships needed to support our philanthropic activities.	1	2	3	4	5
Family involvement	We have clearly defined whom from the family is involved in our philanthropic activities and what the nature of their involvement is.	1	2	3	4	5
	Family members deliver on the work that they have committed to.	1	2	3	4	5
	Family members are actively engaged in our activities (attend meetings, read newsletters, participate in field visits for our family philanthropy, etc.).	1	2	3	4	5
Partners	We have clearly defined which partners are involved in our philanthropic activities and what the nature of their involvement is.	1	2	3	4	5
	We create and maintain productive relationships with our external partners.	1	2	3	4	5

Theme/ dimension in the navigator	Questions	1 Strongly disagree	2 Disagree	3 Neutral	4 Agree	5 Strongly agree
ORGANIZATION	The organizational setup of our giving is clearly defined and provides the necessary direction to our work.	1	2	3	4	5
Resources	The type and amount of resources we deploy are sufficient and appropriate for the results we wish to achieve.	1	2	3	4	5
Governance	Our governance structure is effective and enables us to deliver the most value for our beneficiaries.	1	2	3	4	5
	We have transparent and fair processes to govern our giving and for taking effective decisions.	1	2	3	4	5
Impact	We achieve great impact with what we give.	1	2	3	4	5
	We diligently track our progress against our stated objectives.	1	2	3	4	5

Activity

Learning

Theme/ dimension in the navigator	Questions	1 Strongly disagree	2 Disagree	3 Neutral	4 Agree	5 Strongly agree
LEARNING	We regularly review our giving to ensure that it is aligned with our philanthropic purpose.	1 ◯	2 ◯	3 ◯	4 ◯	5 ◯
	Learning helps us to remain cutting edge in our giving.	1 ◯	2 ◯	3 ◯	4 ◯	5 ◯

Open Questions

What is one aspect of your philanthropy that you would like to preserve?

_____

_____

_____

What is one aspect of your philanthropy that you would like to change?

_____

_____

_____

Do the various dimensions from your navigator align or is there any inconsistency?

_____

_____

_____

Step 2

Review and compare the results with your family members. Identify similarities and differences in your responses.

These evaluations are subjective measures indicating the feeling and thoughts of each individual. However, if you have alignment amongst family members on a specific item, it could provide a reliable indication as to whether things are going well or could be improved.

1. If you have different points of views on certain aspects, we advise you to engage in an open and constructive discussion on that matter.
2. If you collectively gave a certain dimension a high score (4 or 5), then this item seems to be one of your strengths.
3. If you collectively gave a certain dimension a low score (1 or 2), then this item seems to be one of your weaknesses. These points should then be discussed and addressed, as you collectively seem to think that something needs to change.

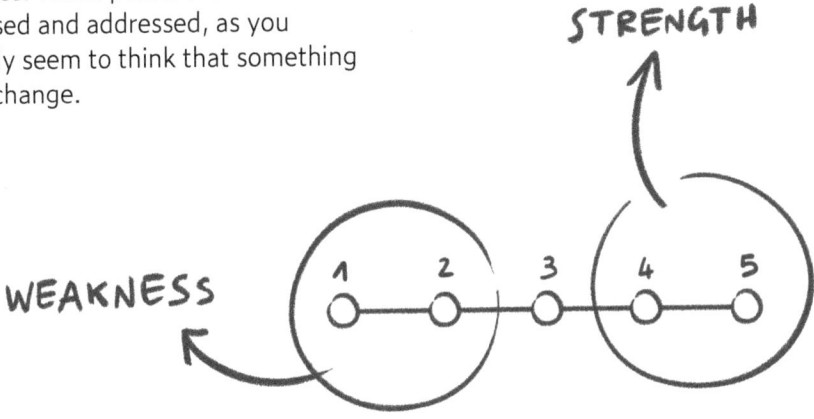

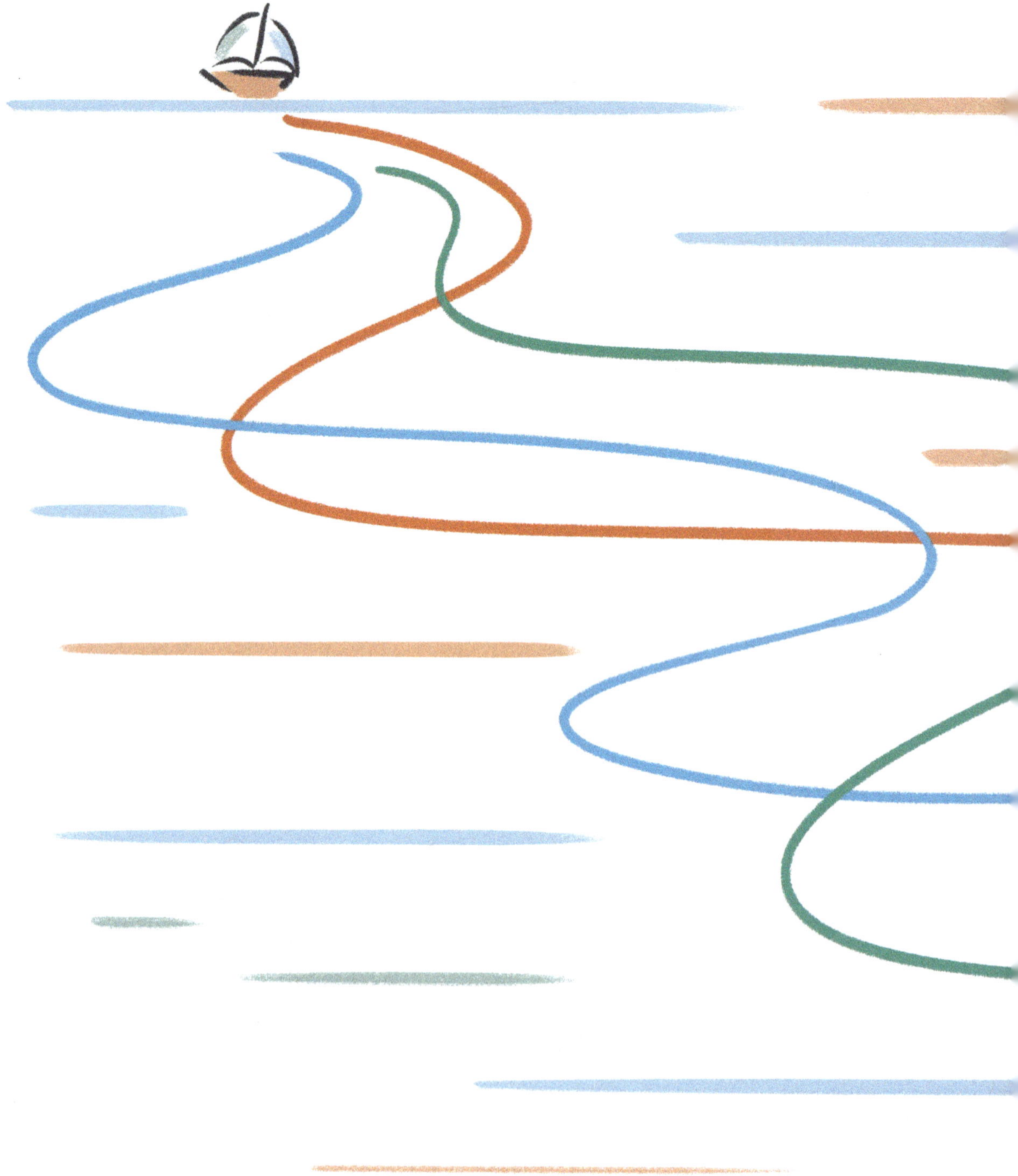

Beyond the Navigator

212 **Beyond the Navigator**

216 **The Making of the Book**

Beyond the Navigator

Beyond the Navigator

Chart Your Course

You have now completed our guided exploration of your giving with the *Family Philanthropy Navigator*. We hope that you have found the book and toolkit to be accessible, helpful and inspiring in informing and shaping your family's journey in giving.

As the world changes rapidly and humanity's challenges grow ever more complex, our ultimate aim through the navigator has been to help families become more effective and efficient in their philanthropy so that they can achieve their goals in an impactful way. With the face of philanthropy also constantly in flux, we hope this book and toolkit has provided both a steady anchor and a reliable compass for your ship.

It is our aspiration that, upon completion of this book, you will have formulated clear answers on the most important questions pertaining to your giving journey:

→ What is the purpose of our philanthropic journey, including motivation, focus and ambition?
→ Which relationships do we need to build in order to power our giving, including family members and partners?
→ How do we wish to organize our philanthropic giving, including resources, governance and impact?
→ How can we embrace the notion of learning into our giving journey in order to get the most out of our successes and setbacks?

These clarifications and decisions will form the foundation and fuel for what comes next. There is only so much preparation, reflection and fine-tuning you can do. At some point, you have to put your model and ideas to the test in the real world. After all, philanthropy is about taking action to make a difference – for the world and for your family. You may not always get it right, and your purpose, relationships and organization can change, but it is now time to make your move.

This is the exciting part. For aspiring philanthropists, having studied the maps, chosen your crew and stocked up for the voyage, it is time to set the compass, chart your course and launch into the fresh waters. For established philanthropists, you are now ready to adjust your course towards new horizons with a fresh perspective.

As you move forward in giving, you may discover that you want or need to change direction, from a slight nudge on the rudder to a hard, sharp turn. We believe the navigator will prove a reliable guide and pilot for any philanthropic family at any stage of their journey in giving – not just as a tool to navigate and establish the first steps but also as a means to take stock of your voyage with a view to making any necessary adjustments or wholesale changes that you might need.

Please remember that the needs of your beneficiaries may change and evolve over time. In fact, everything could change – from the causes you support to your business and family. We, therefore, recommend that you plan to revisit the *Family Philanthropy Navigator* in a structured way with your family at regular intervals in the future, depending on what might work for your circumstances.

This could be a regular review of the core elements of the navigator to make sure you are on track and aligned with your initial conclusions. It could be a comprehensive annual or biannual exercise to work through each step of the navigator from scratch as a 360° health check of your giving. You could also take a deep dive into one aspect of the navigator, such as governance, family involvement or focus, if you feel that it is necessary or if something has changed that requires a new direction.

Beyond the Navigator

A Call to Action

For now, the best way to take your navigator insights and bring them to life is through the creation of an action plan for you and your core team. This will provide the structure and deliverables that will keep you on track.

There are many ways to build an action plan, and many existing, proven models out there. Like each aspect of the navigator, there is no right or wrong way to plan ahead. It makes sense to agree on a path forward and design a plan with your family in a way that works for you. However, in doing so, it might be useful to cover the following questions.

> → What actions do you need to perform?
> → What are your priorities, and how do you decide them?
> → What are your timelines and milestones?
> → Who will take charge of which action items?

Bon Voyage!

It has been a pleasure and privilege to accompany you on this trip through the *Family Philanthropy Navigator*. Please do not hesitate to contact us anytime you have questions or wish to discuss your giving journey. We wish you all the best as you depart from our harbor and head for the horizon. May your journey in giving be rewarding, enjoyable and impactful for you and your family.

Beyond the Navigator

The Making of the Book

FROM SEPTEMBER 2017

Ideation

Context

In 2017, the Swiss biopharmaceutical company Debiopharm pledged to create the Debiopharm Chair for Family Philanthropy at IMD business school in Lausanne with a donation of several million Swiss francs over 15 years. In September that same year, Professor Peter Vogel was chosen to take up the Debiopharm Chair for Family Philanthropy. Shortly after, Dr Małgorzata Kurak joined the Chair as Research Fellow.

The aim of the Chair is to increase the social and financial impact of family philanthropy. In order to achieve the Chair's vision and mission, the idea of creating the *Family Philanthropy Navigator* came to life.

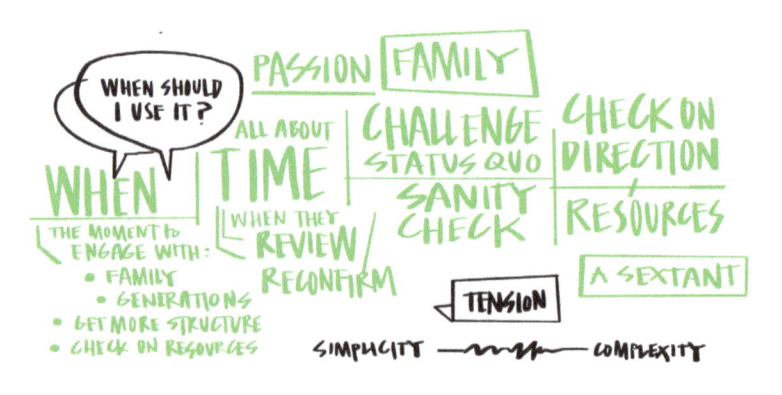

Be clear on the why, for you and for them

Keep the momentum

Integrate feedback but trust your instincts. Only you know the impact you want to achieve.

Organise more cleanly your own process

Iterate quickly

Clarify target audience

Free up time for creativity → delegate other things

Keep it simple and practical

When should I use it?
WHEN — the moment to engage with:
• Family
• Generations
• Get more structure
• Check on resources

All about TIME — when they REVIEW / RECONFIRM
PASSION — FAMILY
CHALLENGE STATUS QUO
SANITY CHECK
CHECK ON DIRECTION + RESOURCES
A SEXTANT
TENSION
SIMPLICITY ——— COMPLEXITY

"If one does not know to which port one is sailing, no wind is favorable."
— SENECA

216 Family Philanthropy Navigator

Timeline

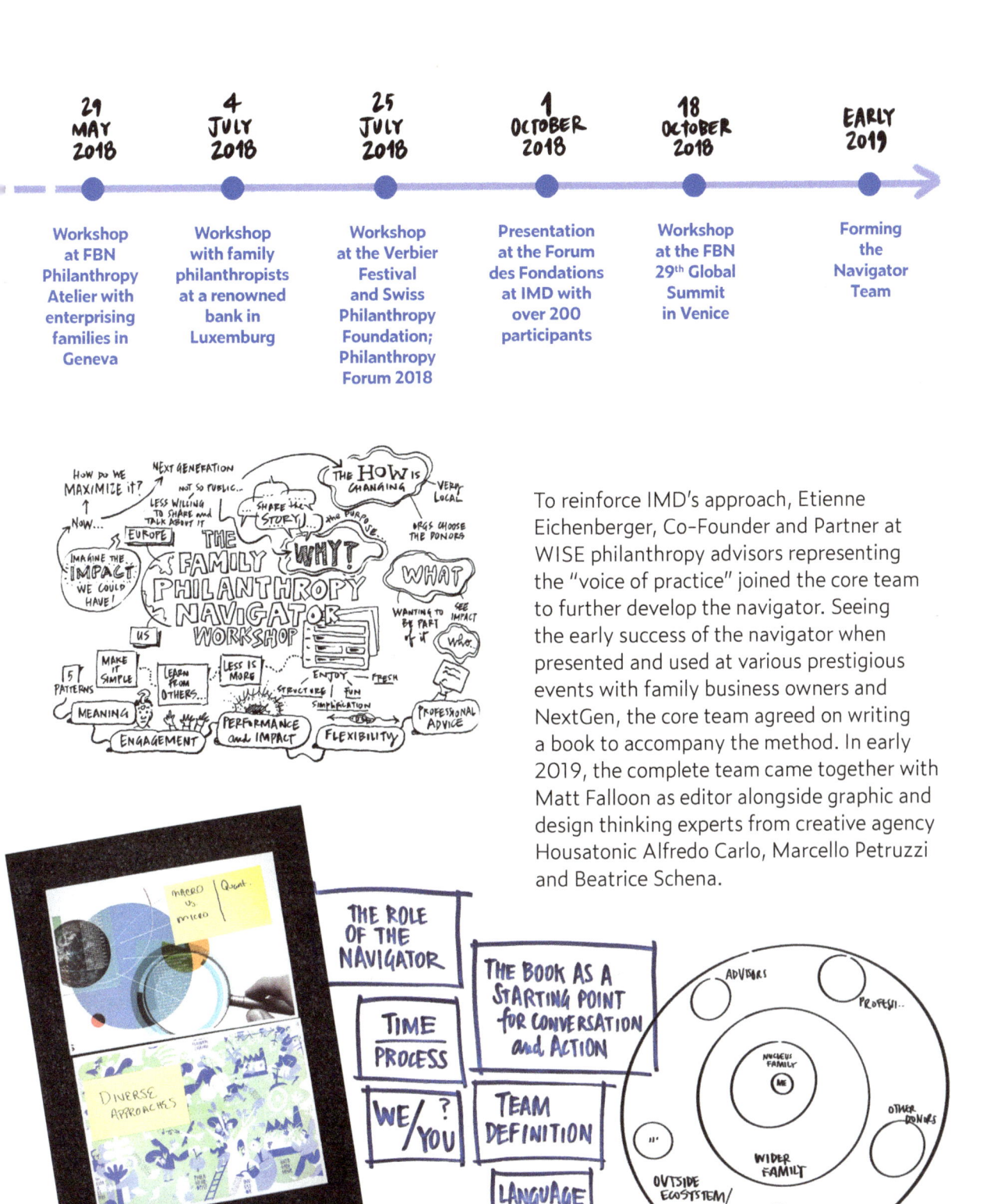

- **29 May 2018** — Workshop at FBN Philanthropy Atelier with enterprising families in Geneva
- **4 July 2018** — Workshop with family philanthropists at a renowned bank in Luxemburg
- **25 July 2018** — Workshop at the Verbier Festival and Swiss Philanthropy Foundation; Philanthropy Forum 2018
- **1 October 2018** — Presentation at the Forum des Fondations at IMD with over 200 participants
- **18 October 2018** — Workshop at the FBN 29th Global Summit in Venice
- **Early 2019** — Forming the Navigator Team

To reinforce IMD's approach, Etienne Eichenberger, Co-Founder and Partner at WISE philanthropy advisors representing the "voice of practice" joined the core team to further develop the navigator. Seeing the early success of the navigator when presented and used at various prestigious events with family business owners and NextGen, the core team agreed on writing a book to accompany the method. In early 2019, the complete team came together with Matt Falloon as editor alongside graphic and design thinking experts from creative agency Housatonic Alfredo Carlo, Marcello Petruzzi and Beatrice Schena.

The Making of the Book

FROM MARCH 2019	4 SEPTEMBER 2019	5 NOVEMBER 2019	7 NOVEMBER 2019	15-17 JANUARY 2020
Leading the research on family philanthropy with FBN	The Family Philanthropy Navigator Workshop with practitioners and partners at IMD	Team workshop at IMD	Philanthropy event at Debiopharm in Lausanne	Team retreat in Grindelwald

Key Audience

→ Aspiring and established philanthropists
→ Families and business owners
→ Individuals and entrepreneurs
→ NextGens
→ Philanthropy experts

Purpose

The aim of the navigator is to help budding and active philanthropists gain clarity so that they can give and structure their approach to giving in more effective ways, and to enable individuals or families to make a long-lasting difference.

Process

The process of designing the navigator and writing the book was driven by design thinking and was very interactive.
On several occasions, we engaged with philanthropists and practitioners for insights and feedback. The navigator is designed to reduce complexity and to provide philanthropists with a snapshot of the various approaches to giving.

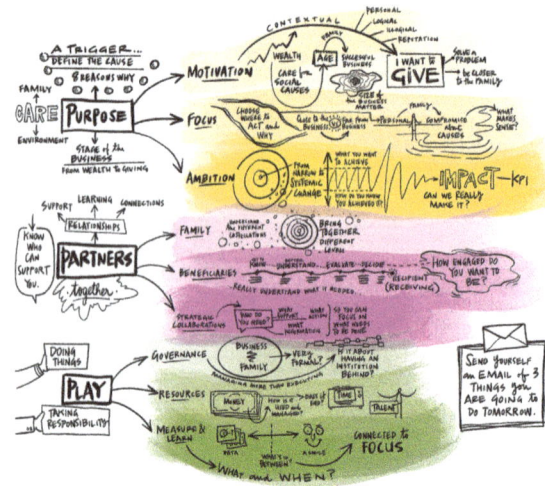

218 Family Philanthropy Navigator

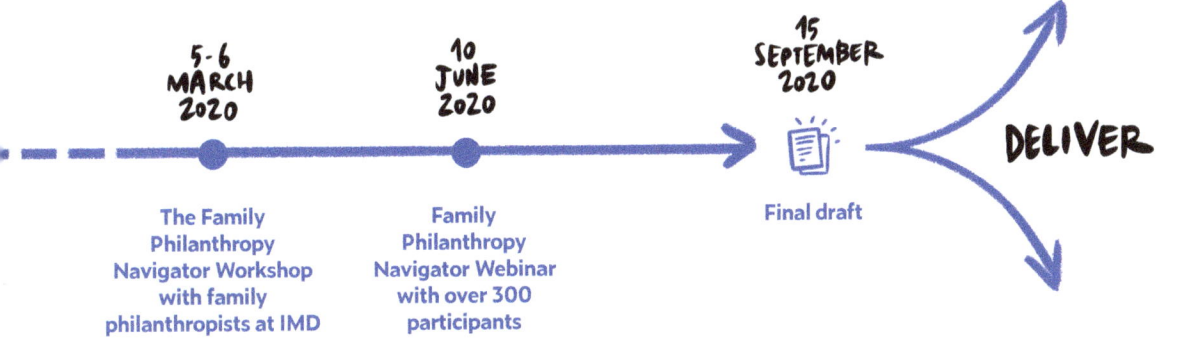

5-6 March 2020 — The Family Philanthropy Navigator Workshop with family philanthropists at IMD

10 June 2020 — Family Philanthropy Navigator Webinar with over 300 participants

15 September 2020 — Final draft

DELIVER

Promise

Using the navigator, as we describe in the book, will help you start a conversation about giving with your family. It is a clear starting point for practical discussions, and for diluting or channeling emotions. Beyond this, it stimulates dialogue between the important stakeholders of your giving such as your external partners and beneficiaries. As a final step, it will help you highlight any challenges in the implementation of your giving.

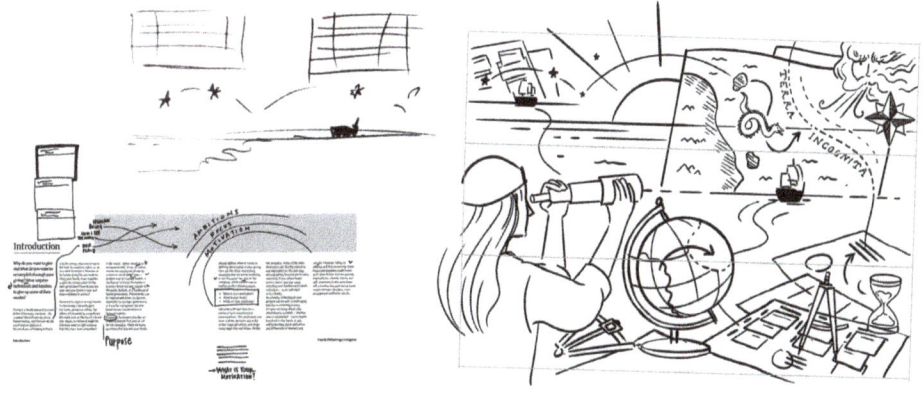

The Making of the Book 219

ABOUT THE AUTHORS

Peter Vogel is Professor of Family Business and Entrepreneurship and the Director of IMD's Global Family Business Center. He holds the Debiopharm Chair for Family Philanthropy at IMD and a PhD in Entrepreneurship from EPFL.

Etienne Eichenberger is Co-Founder and Managing Partner of WISE philanthropy advisors. He serves as Chairman of the Swiss Philanthropy Foundation and on the Advisory Board for the Debiopharm Chair for Family Philanthropy at IMD.

Małgorzata Kurak is a Postdoctoral Research Fellow at the Debiopharm Chair for Family Philanthropy at IMD. She holds a PhD in Economics, Management and Organization from Universitat Autònoma de Barcelona.

IMD
REAL LEARNING. REAL IMPACT

The Institute for Management Development (IMD) is an independent academic institution with Swiss roots and global reach, founded almost 75 years ago by business leaders for business leaders. Since its creation, IMD has been a pioneering force in developing leaders who transform organizations and contribute to society.

Based in Lausanne (Switzerland) and Singapore, IMD has been ranked in the top three of the annual FT's Executive Education Global Ranking for the last nine consecutive years and in the top five for 17 consecutive years. Our MBA and EMBA programs have repeatedly been singled out among the best in Europe and the world.

We believe that this consistency at the forefront of our industry is grounded in IMD's unique approach to creating "Real Learning. Real Impact". Led by an expert and diverse faculty, we strive to be the trusted learning partner of choice for ambitious individuals and organizations worldwide. Challenging what is and inspiring what could be.

We have made a deliberate choice to print this book on demand. Traditional offset requires printing of large quantities and the unsold copies must be destroyed.

This results in serious consequences in terms of carbon footprint: waste of paper and energy, unnecessary greenhouse emissions.

This book is printed on paper sourced by environmentally responsible suppliers to reduce its impact on our earth.